I Saw a Mountain

We are the shoes, we are the last
witnesses.

We are shoes from grandchildren and
grandfathers,

From Prague, Paris and Amsterdam,
And because we are only made of fabric
and leather

And not of blood and flesh, each one of
us avoided the hellfire.

—Moshe Szulsztein, Yiddish poet

*This poem hangs in the United States Holocaust Memorial
Museum in the exhibit of shoes reproduced on the jacket of this
book. Before victims were gassed at the killing centers, the
Nazis took all their belongings from them. This yielded
mountains of clothing. Auschwitz-Birkenau and Majdanek
together generated nearly three hundred thousand pairs of
shoes.*

Bearing Witness

Stories of the Holocaust

Selected by

Hazel Rochman and **Darlene Z. McCampbell**

Orchard Books
New York

Orchard Books
95 Madison Avenue
New York, NY 10016

Manufactured in the United States of America
Book design by Chris Hammill Paul

10 9 8 7 6 5 4 3 2 1

The text of this book is set in 13 point Garamond No. 3.

Library of Congress Cataloging-in-Publication Data

Bearing witness : stories of the Holocaust / selected by Hazel Rochman and Darlene Z. McCampbell.
    p. cm.
    Includes bibliographical references.
    Summary: Offers a multifaceted view of the Holocaust, from a child's bewilderment at having to wear a star and later go into hiding, to the agony of the camps themselves.
    ISBN 0-531-09488-X.—ISBN 0-531-08788-3 (lib. bdg.)
    1. Holocaust, Jewish (1939–1945)—Literary collections.
  2. Holocaust, Jewish (1939–1945)—Personal narratives.
  3. Holocaust, Jewish (1939–1945)—Juvenile literature.
  [1. Holocaust, Jewish (1939–1945)—Literary collections.
  2. Holocaust, Jewish (1939–1945)—Personal narratives.]
  I. Rochman, Hazel. II. McCampbell, Darlene Z.
PN6071.H713B424 1995
808'.8'0358—dc20   95-13352

The Nazis came first for the Communists.
But I wasn't a Communist, so I didn't
speak up. Then they came for the Jews,
but I wasn't a Jew, so I didn't speak up.
Then they came for the trade unionists,
but I wasn't a trade unionist so I didn't
speak up. Then they came for the
Catholics, but I was a Protestant so I
didn't speak up. Then they came for me.
By that time there was no one left.

—Parson Martin Niemöller

Some major Nazi concentration camps and extermination camps
(Camps — labor, transit, concentration, and extermination —
totaled approximately 2,000.)

■ = camp
● = city

Contents

Introduction

The Holocaust was the deliberate, systematic massacre of the Jews of Europe by Hitler and Nazi Germany. Nearly six million Jews were murdered, only because they were Jews. Five million Gentiles, including Gypsies, homosexuals, the disabled, Jehovah's Witnesses, Russians, Polish Catholics, and political prisoners, were also killed.

How could the Holocaust happen? Who is guilty? Could it happen again? Could it have happened to my friend? To me? What would I have done? More than half a century after the end of World War II, survivors, writers, and artists continue to ask these questions with haunting intensity.

Through both fiction and nonfiction, the stories in this anthology give a human face to the statistics about millions. These writers show what happened to ordinary people in many countries of Europe under the Nazis—in homes and crowded ghettos, on the transports, in the death camps, to those who died and to those who survived.

First there was the nightmare invasion of daily life. Ida Vos in *Hide and Seek* dramatizes the bewilderment of a Jewish child who doesn't understand why she has to wear a yellow star. What does it mean, "going into hiding"? Mumford's poem "The White Rose" is about a German Gentile teenager, Sophie Scholl, who was hanged for her resistance to the Nazis. The Gentile boy in *Friedrich* sees what the Nazis do to his Jewish friend. Isabella Leitner remembers how she and her family were taken from their home in Hungary and crammed into a cattle car bound for Auschwitz.

In the pieces about the camps—Spiegelman's comic strip, Levi's memoir, Lanzmann's filmscript, Ozick's short story—each artist finds his or her own way to confront the horror. Levi also shows the role of the Righteous Gentiles, those who risked their lives to save others, even in the camps.

The survivor stories move back and forth between memory and a haunted present. In *New Lives* a Polish woman in New York City remembers herself as a teenager trying to go to school while holed up in the Lodz ghetto. In *Nightfather* a father can't forget the hanging of his Gypsy friend. In Ida Fink's "Splinter" a boy is tormented by guilt that he allowed his mother to save him. As World War II ends, an American GI writes a letter home to his wife about what he has seen in a death camp in Austria.

To read more about the Holocaust and its roots in history, you can turn to the books listed in the bibliography. We hope you will be inspired to move beyond the selections in this anthology to the larger works from which many are drawn.

Was the Holocaust unique? If we say every form of cruelty and oppression is a holocaust, that lessens the enormity of what Hitler called his Final Solution. But there is no hierarchy of suffering. Millions of non-Jews in Europe died for their opposition to Nazism. And mass persecution did not begin or end with the Nazis. Slavery is an abomination that has affected millions. Many Indian nations in the

Americas were decimated as Europeans colonized two continents. In 1915 the Turkish government massacred as many as 1.5 million Armenians. In Cambodia in the 1970s about two million people died at the hands of the Khmer Rouge communists. And "ethnic cleansing" is still happening, in Rwanda, in Bosnia, and elsewhere.

Holocaust survivor Elie Wiesel, in his speech at the opening of the United States Holocaust Memorial Museum, calls for us to remember the dead: "Though not all victims were Jewish, all Jews were victims." He also cries out about ethnic cleansing today: "We cannot tolerate the excruciating sights of this old new war."

The stories in this anthology don't exploit the violence. They don't sensationalize. And they don't offer slick comfort either. In English and in voices translated from many languages, in fiction, memoir, poetry, comic strip, vignette, letter, and filmscript, each writer finds a form to give voice to the unspeakable. Reading about the Holocaust is disturbing. There is no happy ending.

Darlene Zimmerman McCampbell
Growing Up in Chicago

When I hear the name Kielce now, the town in Poland where my father was born, I think of the Jewish people killed during the Holocaust. I also know Kielce was a place where there was a pogrom, a massacre of Jews, *after* the war. But when I was growing up, Kielce meant something very different.

I knew my Jewish relatives left eastern Europe around World War I. They left Poland and Russia and the Ukraine because Jews were persecuted and life there was hard. But, to me, that didn't seem so unlike stories I had heard about life in America. My father was selling brushes on the streets of Chicago at the age of thirteen. He dropped out of school to help support his family.

My family and friends vacationed at "the farm" in Kibbie, Michigan, where I spent my first ten summers. That summer world was filled with water pumps and outhouses, fresh sweet corn and wild blackberries, old people from Pinsk and Kiev, kids my age from Chicago.

And I remember picnics with the "Kielcers," the whole community of Jewish refugees born in Kielce, Poland, who formed a club in the new country named after their birthplace. The Kielcers were old people with white hair and heavy accents. I grew up with the name Kielce. Kielce was where my father was born and where my grandfather died. It was where so many of the people I knew were from. That was all it meant to me then.

Only later did I realize how lucky my family had been to leave eastern Europe before the Nazis came into power. As the Nazi commander tells in the interview from *Shoah* on page 70 of this book, trainloads of people were sent from Kielce to the camps. The Kielcers who came to this country lived. Those who stayed did not.

Hazel Rochman

Growing Up in Johannesburg

While I was growing up in South Africa, I read a lot about the Holocaust. It seemed very close, my worst nightmares come true. What if "they" suddenly invaded my comfortable home and dragged me and my parents away?

Like Darlene's family, my grandparents left eastern Europe around the turn of the century to escape hard times and anti-Semitism. Some of my relatives went to America, but my grandparents traveled steerage on a boat to South Africa. My father was three years old.

Some stayed behind in the Old Country. During the Holocaust, my husband's grandmother and aunt were herded by the Nazis into the Vilna ghetto, where they died. One uncle was shot to death. Another has never been heard from. When a third uncle returned to his home in Poland after the war, he was chased out by the new owners. He emigrated to Israel.

During World War II, when I was a child, there was a strong pro-Nazi movement in South Africa. My father made secret arrangements to hide me with a Gentile family if the anti-Semites gained power. In fact, the pro-Nazis did become the apartheid government after the war. However, the people they persecuted were not the Jews, but the Blacks. It took me a long time to realize that my nightmares were happening to the people around me.

Racism was the law. They called it *apartheid* (pronounced A-PART-HATE), which is Afrikaans for apartness, or separate development. There was no deliberate genocide, but hunger, prison, family separation, torture, and exile were common experience. Apartheid was sanctified by the Dutch Reformed Church. The whites told themselves they had a divine mission to care for the inferior blacks and to defend racial purity against "barbarism." A system of laws was introduced that made Africans foreigners in their own country. If you were black, you had to carry a pass, a document that showed you had permission to work in a white area, and you had to produce your pass for any policeman.

This is how Mark Mathabane describes a pass raid on

his home and neighborhood in *Kaffir Boy: The True Story of a Black Youth's Coming of Age in Apartheid South Africa.*

A huge throng of handcuffed black men and women, numbering in the hundreds, filled the narrow streets from side to side. The multitude, murmuring like herds of restless cattle, was being marched by scores of black policemen and a dozen or so white ones, some of whom had fierce police dogs on leashes, toward a row of about ten police vans and trucks parked farther down the street. More handcuffed men and women were still filing out of the yards on either side, swelling the ranks of those already choking the streets. It seemed as if the entire population of Alexandra had been arrested.

That scene in Alexandra was happening barely five miles from my home on a tree-lined Johannesburg street.

For the Dead and the Living

by Elie Wiesel

Elie Wiesel, a Holocaust survivor, is an
author and Nobel Peace Prize winner.
This essay is adapted from the speech he
gave in 1993 at the dedication ceremony
of the United States Holocaust Memorial
Museum in Washington, D.C.

With the exception of Israel, ours is the one country that
has seen fit to make preserving the memory of the Holocaust
a national imperative. When President Jimmy Carter set
up the Presidential Commission on the Holocaust in 1978
and appointed me chairman, I was asked about my vision
of the future Holocaust Museum. I wrote one sentence,
now permanently inscribed on one of its walls: "For the
dead and the living, we must bear witness." For not only

are we responsible for the memories of the dead, we are also responsible for what we do with those memories.

Words, images, sounds—that is the stuff of memory. Fifty years ago, somewhere in the Carpathian Mountains, a young Jewish woman read in a Hungarian newspaper a brief account of the Warsaw Ghetto uprising. Astonished, dismayed, she wondered aloud: "Why are our Jews in Warsaw behaving like this? Why are they fighting? Couldn't they have waited quietly until the end of the war?"

Treblinka, Ponar, Belzec, Chelmno, Birkenau; she had never heard of those places. One year later, together with her entire family, she was in a cattle car traveling to the Black Hole of History named Auschwitz.

But those places, and others, were known to officials in Washington and London, Moscow and Stockholm, Geneva and the Vatican. After all, by April 1943 nearly 4 million Jews had already perished. The Pentagon knew, the State Department knew, the White House knew, most governments knew; only the victims did not know. Thus the painful question: Why weren't Hungarian Jews, the last remnant of eastern European Jewry, warned of their impending doom?

Jews of every description—old and young, beggars and industrialists, sages and madmen, Ashkenazim from France and Sephardim from Greece, intellectuals from Lithuania and Hasidim from Poland—together began their inexorable journey to a fiery altar of unprecedented dimension. I saw them all, including the children, entering the shadow of flames.

Light is God's shadow, said Giordano Bruno, the Italian philosopher who was burned at the stake in Rome four centuries ago. I say: No. It is *fire* that is His shadow, the fire that consumed a third of a people whose memory of God is the most ancient in recorded history.

Inside the Kingdom of Night, we tried to understand and could not. We found ourselves in an unfamiliar world, a creation parallel to God's, with its own hierarchy, its own princes and hangmen, its own laws and customs. There were only two categories: those who were there to kill and those who were there to be killed.

In Poland, SS officers used Jewish infants for target practice. The only emotion they ever showed was anger when they missed.

In Kiev, an SS officer beheaded two Jewish children in front of their mother. In her anguish, she held them close and began to dance.

In Romania, the Iron Guard killed Jews and displayed them in butcher shops with signs: "Kosher Meat."

As you walk through the Holocaust Museum, as you look into the eyes of the killers and their victims, ask yourselves: How could the murderers do what they did and go on living? Why was Berlin encouraged in its belief that it could decree with impunity the humiliation, persecution, extermination of an entire people? Why weren't the railways leading to Birkenau bombed by Allied planes? Why was there no outcry, no public indignation?

Another question: Where did the poorly armed fighters in the ghettos and the forests find the courage to take on the mightiest legions in Europe?

And the most awesome question of all: Why was man's silence matched by God's?

The questions, in fact, are endless and will forever remain unanswered. Indeed, if there is an answer to the Holocaust, it must—by definition—be the wrong answer. Nor is the Museum an answer; it is but a question mark.

Every event connected with that period defies human understanding. It is not because I cannot explain, that you will not understand; it is because you will not understand, that I cannot explain.

The essence of this tragedy is that it can never be fully communicated.

In one of my tales, an SS officer derides a young yeshiva student, telling him that if he happened to survive, his words would fall on deaf ears: "Some will laugh at you," he says. "Others will try to redeem themselves through you. . . . People will refuse to believe you. You will possess the truth; but it will be the truth of a madman."

And yet, we are duty-bound to try. Not to do so would mean to forget. To forget would mean to kill the victims a second time. We could not prevent their first death; we must not allow them to vanish again. Memory is not only a victory over time, it is also a triumph over injustice.

That is one of the lessons we have learned. There are others. We have learned that though the Holocaust was principally a Jewish tragedy, its implications are universal. Though not all victims were Jewish, all Jews were victims. We have learned that whatever happens to one community ultimately affects every community. Anti-Semitism is the beginning, not the end, of a disease. Prejudice knows no boundaries. When children are killed in Bosnia, it is our humanity that has failed. When people massacre one another in India, it is our fault too. We have learned that although every human being has the right to be different, none has the right to be indifferent to suffering.

Nevertheless, hatred continues to cause so much suffering in the world today. Religious hatred, ethnic hatred, racial hatred.

Let us therefore seize this moment to condemn the

scourge of anti-Semitism, bigotry, and hatred. The bloodshed in Bosnia has to be stopped. We cannot tolerate the excruciating sights of this old new war. I was in the former Yugoslavia last fall. I cannot sleep remembering what I have seen. As a Jew I am saying that we have to do something to stop the killing in that country. People fight each other and children die. Why? Something—anything—must be done to stop the bloodshed there. It will not stop unless we stop it.

Remember the loving yet naïve woman, somewhere in the Carpathians, who together with most Jews of her town perished in a tempest of fury and fire?

She was my mother.

from

Hide and Seek

by Ida Vos

Translated from the Dutch by Terese

Edelstein and Inez Smidt, these three

vignettes are taken from Vos's

autobiographical story about a young

child's experience under Nazi occupation

in Holland.

Would You Like a Star, Too?

Today for the first time Rachel must go to school with a yellow star on her coat, a big yellow star, with the word *Jew* written in the middle of it. Thus everyone can see that she is Jewish. The Germans have ordered the wearing of the star, and Rachel finds it horrible.

All her mother did yesterday evening was sew stars on their clothing. "I see stars," Mother said, and they even had to laugh about it.

"I'll take you to the tram," says Papa. "Come on, hurry up, otherwise you'll be late for school."

They put their coats on. How big the star is. Esther's star is even bigger than Rachel's. "It looks that way because Esther has such a small body," their father explains. "That's why her star seems larger."

When they arrive at the tram stop they see many other people with stars on, grown-up people and little people. "All Jews," an old man says. "Yesterday I did not know they were Jews, although I suspected they were."

"You must hold your schoolbag under your arm as you usually do, not against your star," Father admonishes her.

Rachel blushes. Father saw that she was trying to hide her star.

"It's difficult, but if you don't hide your star now, you'll get over the embarrassment more quickly. When the war is over, we'll make a huge fire and we'll throw all the stars of the whole world into it."

"Boy, will that stink!" Rachel exclaims.

"It stinks right now," Leo says. "I smelled the star when I put my coat on."

"Children, here comes the tram," Father calls.

The moment has come. For the first time Rachel will have to go on the tram with that horrible star.

"Come in!" the driver of the tram calls out to them. "It really is springtime in my tram now. All these children with yellow daffodils on their coats. I wish I could wear one."

When they are all inside, many people begin to clap, just as an audience does at the end of a play. Rachel does not understand. A man nudges her. "Bow, the clapping is for you, for your stars."

Rachel does not dare to move. What is that? Are the people clapping for that big yellow star?

The children look at one another. "They are clapping for us," Leo says, and he begins to bow. "Thank you, people. Thank you very much."

A few people do not clap, but look straight ahead instead. Leo approaches one of those people. "Ma'am, would you like a star, too? Tomorrow I'll bring you one. Would you like a star, too, mister?"

"Go away, you little Jew boy," the man replies, and to the woman sitting next to him he says, "You can't cut them down to size. Not the big Jews and not the little ones, either."

Going into Hiding

"This is Mrs. Helsloot," says Mother. "She has come to take you. You are going into hiding."

"Going into hiding?" Rachel doesn't know what her mother means. "I'm not going with her," she replies.

"My dear, you must."

"Why haven't Papa and you told us? And what does 'going into hiding' mean?" Rachel asks.

"Going into hiding is this: You hide from the Germans," her mother explains. "It is becoming too dangerous to wait here at home until they come get us. Go along. Esther and you will sleep one night at Mrs. Helsloot's. Tomorrow she will bring you to a village nearby. Papa and I will be there, too. Come, dear, get your scooter and go along." Mother says it in such a special way that Rachel has to listen.

"Remember your scooter," says Mrs. Helsloot. "It is for Anke. You can't use it for the time being, anyway."

"Who is Anke?" asks Rachel.

"She is my little daughter. You'll see her when we're home," Mrs. Helsloot answers.

"Where are we going?" asks Esther.

"I can't tell you," says Mrs. Helsloot. "Imagine that the Germans should arrest us and ask you where you're going. It really is better that you don't know."

Rachel doesn't understand a single thing that Mrs. Helsloot says. After all, it has happened so suddenly.

"Go now." Mother gives Rachel a kiss. "I'll give your love to Papa later. Tomorrow we'll see each other again."

Rachel kisses her mother and they go. She and Esther are on the scooter, and Mrs. Helsloot is walking next to them.

A German flag is hanging from the house on the corner. Under the flag two children are busily eating. It is Lotte and Elly. They are celebrating Hitler's birthday.

"Tomorrow is Hitler's birthday," Lotte said yesterday. "We are going to eat delicious cakes and you're not getting any."

"Keep going! Don't look back!" calls Mrs. Helsloot.

After ten minutes they are walking in a street where they have never been before. "Stand still. Something important is going to happen now," says Mrs. Helsloot.

The woman reaches into her coat pocket. She takes out a scissors and goes toward Esther and Rachel with it.

Rachel feels her star being pulled. She feels Mrs. Helsloot cutting threads. "Don't!" she cries out. "We're not allowed to walk outside without a star. We'll be picked up then." She wants to stop Mrs. Helsloot, but the woman is holding her hand.

"Rachel, from now on you must do what I say," Mrs. Helsloot informs her, "at least if you don't want to be picked up. You're not allowed to walk about *with* a star now."

Mrs. Helsloot continues cutting. With one more pull she has the yellow patch in her hand. They are standing by a sewer. The star disappears into it. Now it is Esther's turn. Esther doesn't mind it so much. Quietly she lets Mrs. Helsloot go about her work.

"Come, children, we'll go on."

The girls step on the scooter again. Esther is standing in front, Rachel in back.

"Goodness!" exclaims Mrs. Helsloot, and she puts a hand over her mouth. "Look at that, Rachel!" The woman points to her coat, where the star was. "You can see exactly where that rotten star was. The rest of your coat is lighter blue than the place where your star was. Esther, make sure that your head remains in front of Rachel's chest."

Rachel is terrified. Her hands are sweaty and her heart is beating in her throat. She wants to go home to Papa and Mama. She does *not* want to go into hiding at all. Imagine that some Germans should come and see that blue patch.

"Heinz," one German would say to another. "This child has taken off her star, and that's not allowed. We'll arrest her."

After they have been walking for fifteen minutes, Mrs. Helsloot says: "Here we are. Go inside quickly."

They come into a house where three girls and a man are sitting at a table. "This is my husband and these are my children," Mrs. Helsloot says.

"Hello, Mr. Helsloot." Rachel and Esther shake hands with Mrs. Helsloot's husband.

"Take your coat off," says the man. "My God, Tine, how did you dare to walk so with that child? She has a star on, a blue one."

"I know that," Mrs. Helsloot explains to her husband. "Luckily it went all right. I'll try to bleach that blue star this evening. I'll get that imprint out."

"I hope so," says Mr. Helsloot. He turns to Rachel and Esther. "Would you like a sandwich? Mmm, a hearty sandwich with brown bread and bacon." Bacon? Rachel is already becoming sick just hearing the word *bacon*. Doesn't that man know that Jewish children may not eat bacon?

"Pardon me," Mr. Helsloot apologizes. "I hadn't thought about it. You don't eat pork."

In the evening Mrs. Helsloot brings them to bed. "Sleep tight," she says. "Tomorrow I'll take you to your parents. We'll go on the tram to Delft, and what happens after that you'll see for yourself."

"We haven't been *allowed* to take a tram for a long time," Rachel wants to say, but she sighs and holds her tongue. She is terribly tired from everything.

"I'm going to try to bleach your coat now. Then when we go tomorrow you'll have no star on it—no yellow one and no blue one. Good night."

Each girl receives a kiss from Mrs. Helsloot. "That's nice," Rachel thinks.

The sisters crawl close to each other. It is pleasant to be together in one bed. At home they sleep in separate beds.

"Where are we now?" whispers Esther.

"Wait," Rachel whispers back. "I'll look." Very quietly she gets out of bed. She opens the curtain. On the other side of the street is a little sign with a street name on it. "All . . . ar . . . I can't read it very well."

"Wait, I'll turn the light on," says Esther, and she pulls the little string hanging above the bed.

"Don't! You must never do that again. When you're in hiding you must never turn the light on when the curtains are open. And the curtains—those must never, never be open, for no one must see you!"

Mrs. Helsloot is standing in the room. "You just have to get used to it," she continues. "It will be hard. Don't be so foolish anymore, all right?"

"No, Mrs. Helsloot," the girls say at the same time.

"It is difficult with your coat, but it probably will work," Mrs. Helsloot says.

"And if it doesn't?" Rachel asks her.

"Then you'll have to put that coat on anyway," the woman tells her. "You'll just hold a book in the place where your star was."

Rachel can't sleep. Esther is breathing very quietly next to her. She is sleeping.

Rachel thinks about tomorrow. Perhaps she will have to go outside without a star and yet with a star. How difficult everything is today.

The door opens very softly.

Mrs. Helsloot is standing in front of the bed. "It worked," she whispers. "No one can see that you have had a star on your coat. Sleep well. Good night."

"Good night, Mrs. Helsloot." Rachel sighs. "And give my regards to your husband."

They Aren't Any Different

The second night in hiding is past.

How happy Rachel and Esther were yesterday when they saw their father and mother again. They find it comforting to sleep near their own parents, even if they aren't at home but in a strange house, in a rectory in Schipluiden.

Mrs. Helsloot brought them there. "This is Father Thijssen," she said to the girls. "Shake hands with him."

"Hello, sir," they said to a man in a black robe with a whole lot of buttons on it.

"Hello, children. Welcome to Schipluiden. Your parents are upstairs," Father Thijssen told them.

The Hartogs are all sitting at the table now. "Dora, my housekeeper, and Neeltje, my servant girl, will bring you your breakfast," the priest said when he came to see them very early this morning. "They weren't here when you arrived yesterday. They had the day off, but now you can get acquainted with each other."

"It's just like being on vacation," Mother exclaims. "I don't have to make our own breakfast."

Someone knocks loudly on the door. "Come in," calls Father.

The sound of laughter fills the hall. "You first," Rachel hears. "No, you first. Don't be so silly."

"Come in!" Father calls out again.

"Go on!" Rachel hears.

The door bursts open. Two women enter in single file. One carries a tray, while the other has a teapot in her hand. They remain standing in the room.

"Put the teapot down, Neel," says the woman with the tray. Neel does as she is told and sets the teapot on the table. She gazes intently at Father; then she looks at Mother.

"Dora," she exclaims, "they aren't any different."

"You see," Dora explains, "we've never seen Jews before. That's why it took a while before we dared to come in."

Neeltje runs out of the room. "Enjoy your breakfast," Dora calls, and she runs after Neeltje.

from

The White Rose:
Sophie Scholl 1921–1943

by Erika Mumford

This excerpt, part of a long dramatic
poem, is based on a true story of the
German student resistance movement
called the White Rose, which protested
the Nazi genocide of Jews. The White
Rose was founded in 1942 by Sophie
Scholl, her brother, Hans, and their
friend Christoph Probst. In 1943 they
were caught and executed.

Why must it be me?
 Why not you?
But there are others, political people—
 The work is not political.
people who understand this kind of thing—
 What don't you understand?

organizations—
We are born and die alone.
I don't want to die.
The work is urgent.
Oh please, please don't.
The decision is yours.
I'm so afraid.
Yes.

Breathless, in the streetcar. Beside me
an SS officer fidgets, glances restlessly
about. Once, horribly,
I catch his eye. My briefcase
burns into my side, I can't stop
seeing the clasp give way, papers
spilling, whirling into people's laps—
does it look odd? Too full?
Should I have looked away so quickly?

The ticket collector—
breathe deeply—don't run—I fumble
with change—the briefcase
slips, crashes down, the officer
grabs it   his face swims before my eyes
—hands it back, smiling—
hot trickle of terror down my leg.

There are times at night
when I *am* fear, icy, my bones
liquid, blood humming in darkness

listening. I pray to sleep, I pray
to wake and find myself and Hans,
Christoph and Alex and the others
just students again.
The deadly pressure lifted.

from

Friedrich

by Hans P. Richter

Translated from the German by Edite
Kroll, these two episodes are from a
story of friendship set in Nazi Germany.
A Gentile boy tells of the mounting
persecution of his Jewish friend.

The Cinema
(1940)

JUD SÜSS (Sweet Jew) it said in enormous letters over the
entrance. At both sides, paintings depicted heads of Jews
with beards and earlocks. The film was in its eighth week.
Whole school classes and police divisions marched to it in
unison. Everyone was supposed to have seen it. Because
the war restricted most other entertainment, films were

the most important amusement left. And a picture so many people talked and wrote about tempted everybody.

Friedrich was waiting for me outside a small soap shop. I had once been reprimanded in the Hitler Youth for consorting with a Jew. Since then, we only met in those places where we were unlikely to meet people we knew.

"I looked at the pictures outside," Friedrich told me. "I'm really glad you're going with me. I'd never have dared it alone."

While Friedrich read the reviews exhibited in the showcases, I went to the ticket window. Beneath the price list was an illuminated sign that read NO ONE UNDER 14 ALLOWED.

Sometimes they made you show your ID at the ticket window. But no one asked for it this time. And that's what Friedrich had been so afraid of. Although we were already fifteen, Friedrich only had a Jewish identification card.

"Did you get them?" he asked in a whisper, peering around.

I nodded, pleased. Both tickets in hand, I sauntered slowly towards the entrance, looking very confident I was sure.

Friedrich followed behind me, making certain I was always blocking him from the view of the lady examining tickets.

But she didn't ask for identification either. She didn't even look at us. In a monotone she murmured her "To your left, please" and let us go inside.

Inside the foyer, Friedrich heaved a loud sigh of relief. "I really don't like this stupid cheating. But a film like this is really important for me, isn't it?"

We stepped into the dim theater. An usherette received us and led us to our row.

Friedrich thanked her politely.

The usherette smiled kindly.

We were early, so we got good seats in the center of the row facing the curtain. Only a few people sat in the other seats as yet.

But, nevertheless, Friedrich looked in all directions before sitting down on his folding chair. Then he stretched out his legs and enjoyed the comfortable seat. "Upholstered," he said with pleasure, and stroked the soft armrest.

Meanwhile, a new and older usherette had come in. She took over our side of the cinema, and the younger usherette went over to the other side. She went through our row of seats.

Friedrich jumped up to let her pass.

Again she smiled, gratefully this time.

"Today is the first time since Mother died that I am seeing a film," Friedrich said softly. "And what a film! I'm glad Mother didn't have to live through all that's happened in the last two years. We are suffering, and not just because there's a war on."

Gradually the theater filled up. Seats were taken to the right and left of us. Many young people came to this afternoon performance. The usherettes closed the doors. Everyone waited for the lights to go out.

Suddenly the big ceiling lights went on. Over the loudspeaker a voice announced: "We ask all teenagers to have their ID's ready."

The two usherettes began to go through the rows, starting from opposite ends of the cinema. They glanced briefly at each identification card, sending two or three teenagers out of the cinema. Everything went speedily and quietly.

Friedrich had grown pale. Restlessly, he slid back and forth in his seat. He'd watch the usherettes, and then his eyes would peer along our row.

"What are you getting so nervous about?" I asked, trying to calm him down. "They're only checking to see if we're really fourteen. Just let me handle it; all you have to do is show your ID."

But Friedrich behaved more and more noticeably.

Everyone around us turned to stare.

It embarrassed me.

Finally Friedrich bent close to me. Like a little girl he whispered in my ear. "I kept something from you. We Jews aren't allowed to see films anymore. It's forbidden. If they find me here, I'll be sent to a camp. I must get away. Help me, quick!"

The older usherette was pushing her way through to us.

Friedrich still hesitated.

The usherette came closer.

Friedrich leaped up.

"Stop!" cried the usherette.

Friedrich tried to squeeze through.

The legs of the other people in our row were in the way.

The usherette caught up with him. "I know what you're up to!" she said loudly, addressing the whole room. "When ID's are examined you disappear and hide, and as soon as it gets dark, you slink back!"

I went and stood beside Friedrich.

"Come on, out with it!" the usherette commanded Friedrich. "Then you can go wherever you wish."

"Here it is!" I said, handing her mine.

"I wasn't speaking to you," the usherette said. "It's this one I'm talking to."

"We belong together!" I burst out, but regretted the words the moment I spoke them.

The usherette hadn't been listening.

Friedrich was trembling. His face a dark red, he stammered: "I . . . I . . . I left it at home."

The young usherette had come up from behind. "Why don't you leave the boy in peace!" she suggested. "Don't make such a fuss! It's time anyway!"

Friedrich pleaded: "Please, I want to leave. I'll go voluntarily."

Grinning, the older usherette put her hands on her hips and said, "There's something wrong here, I can tell."

"No, no!" Friedrich protested.

Quick as a flash the usherette grabbed hold of Friedrich's jacket lapels. She put her hand in his pocket. "And what's this here?" she sneered, pulling out the case with Friedrich's ID.

"Give that to me!" Friedrich screamed. "I want my ID!" He tried to tear it out of her hand.

But she just leaned back, grinning, holding the case out of his reach.

Friedrich behaved like someone gone mad.

The younger usherette tried to calm him down.

Meanwhile, her colleague was examining Friedrich's identification card. At once, her face grew serious. Without hesitating, she handed the identification back to him. "Come on!" she ordered.

Friedrich pushed through the row and followed her to the side exit. I stayed behind him.

Everyone's eyes followed us.

By the side exit, the usherette took Friedrich's arm and led him outside. Reproachfully, she said, "You must be tired of life! You must be dying to go to a concentration camp, eh!"

Behind us, the lights went out and the victory fanfares of the weekly newsreel sounded.

Benches
(1940)

Friedrich suddenly appeared in the center of town. "Can you spare me some time? I want to tell you something. My father wouldn't understand, and anyway, he never listens properly anymore. And I have to tell someone, I just have to. Honestly, it won't take long!" Without waiting for my answer, he began to walk beside me.

"It started about four weeks ago," he began. "I was going to collect a pound of noodles which a friend in the suburb had promised us.

"I walked past the old church and through the street with trees—you know, the one where the tram turns left. The trees are all lime trees and they smelled so strongly because they were in bloom then.

"I had got as far as the red brick building. I hadn't been paying attention—just meandering along. That's when I suddenly saw the girl in front of me.

"She had very small feet and black hair. I walked behind her for a long time, closely watching how she set down her feet, moved her head, and how she carried the heavy shopping net.

"There were apples in the net, those with the crinkly skin. How I would have loved one of those apples. 'If one falls out of the net,' I thought, 'I'll speed it away.' I was still picturing this in my mind when the net went *crack* and all the apples rolled into the street.

"The girl turned at once, put her hands to her mouth, and said: 'What a stinking war-net!' She had grey eyes, grey with a bit of blue in them. They looked great with her black hair. She was just beautiful.

"I helped her pick up the apples. We put them back into the net. But the net wouldn't mend properly, so we carried it together to her house.

"Her name's Helga. Her father is a soldier. She works in a kindergarten. That day, her day off, she had gone to the country and swapped hand-knitted potholders for the apples.

"When we got to her door, she looked at me very sweetly and said, 'Thank you. *Auf Wiedersehen!*' She gave me one of the apples as a present. I didn't eat it, though. I'm still saving it—as a memory.

"I quickly ran to our friend and picked up the noodles. On my way home, I walked by the kindergarten and asked when she stopped work at night.

"From then on I stood and waited by the kindergarten every evening. As soon as Helga came out, I'd always walk where she had to see me. And when she'd look at me, I always said hello right away.

"At first, her eyes just grew large. She looked even more beautiful then! The third evening, she began to smile when she saw me. At night I dreamed only of Helga.

"A week later she allowed me to walk her home. I can't tell you how happy that made me! We never said much to each other. It was good just walking side by side. Sometimes Helga even looked at me.

"All Helga knew about me was that my name was Friedrich Schneider, nothing else. And I couldn't tell her anything, otherwise she wouldn't have let me meet her anymore.

"Well, the Sunday before last we had our first date; we were going to meet in the town park. My father had already wondered what I was doing out every evening. But when he saw me getting dressed up, he shook his head and said, 'Think about what you are doing, Friedrich!' That's all he said; he turned away then. But I went all the same.

"The weather was beautiful. The roses were beginning to bloom. The park was fairly empty. Only a few mothers were pushing their prams around.

"Helga wore a dark red dress—with her black hair and those grey eyes. When she looked at me, I could feel it inside me. And those small feet! When I think of it!—

"I had brought Helga a slim volume of poetry. And she was so delighted with it that I felt ashamed.

"We walked through the town park and Helga recited poems. She knew many by heart.

"Again and again I searched out lonely paths, where we would hopefully meet nobody. After we had been walking for a while, Helga wanted to sit down.

"I didn't know what to do. I couldn't really refuse her such a thing. Before I could think of an excuse, we came to one of the green benches and Helga simply sat down.

"I stood in front of the bench, shifting from one foot to the other. I didn't dare sit down. I kept looking to see if anyone was coming.

" 'Why don't you sit down?' Helga asked. But I couldn't think of an answer, so when she said, 'Sit down!' I actually sat down.

"But I wasn't comfortable. What if an acquaintance came by? I slid back and forth on the bench.

"Helga noticed. She took a small bar of chocolate from her handbag and gave me some. I hadn't eaten chocolate for who knows how long, but I couldn't enjoy it; I was much too nervous. I even forgot to say thank you.

"Helga had the little book of poems on her lap. She wasn't reading it; she was looking at me. From time to time she'd ask me something. I can't remember what I replied, because I was so terribly afraid, there on that green bench.

"All at once Helga stood up. She took my arm and pulled me along. We hadn't gone far when we reached a yellow bench, which was marked FOR JEWS ONLY.

"Helga stopped by this bench and said, 'Would it make you feel better if we sat here?'

"I got a shock. 'How do you know?' I asked.

"Helga sat down on the yellow bench and said, 'It occurred to me.' She said that so simply and matter-of-factly!

"But I really couldn't sit on a yellow bench with this girl. I pulled Helga up and took her home. I could have howled with disappointment. The beautiful Sunday gone! But I was much too nervous to go on walking hand in hand and tell her about me.

"But Helga behaved the whole time as if it were natural to go out with a Jew. She told me about her home, about the children in the kindergarten, and about her holidays. And she took my hand and held it tightly. I could have fallen around her neck and wept! But I was much too excited and stupid to do or say anything sensible like that.

"Helga stopped outside her door. She looked long into my eyes. Then she said, 'We'll meet again next Sunday. But we won't go to the town park. Instead we'll go to the country where there are real woods, where they don't have yellow benches!'

"I tried to talk her out of it, but she stopped me with a kiss and was gone into the house.

"I wandered around town all that evening and half the night. I didn't get home until long after curfew. Luckily no one caught me. But Father was quite furious.

"I debated the whole week whether or not to go. When Sunday came I didn't go after all. I couldn't, you see. The girl would be sent to a concentration camp if she were seen with me!"

from

The Big Lie: A True Story
by Isabella Leitner

This excerpt is from Leitner's account of
how she and her family were rounded
up in Hungary and transported to the
Polish death camp Auschwitz. Her
mother and baby sister, Potyó, died
there. Leitner has written more about
her experiences in *Fragments of Isabella:
A Memoir of Auschwitz* (1978) and in
Saving the Fragments (1985).

May twenty-eighth was my birthday, but we had no cele-
bration. That day, a young German soldier came to the
ghetto with a gleaming pistol and a barking dog.

"You will all be ready at 4:00 A.M. for deportation,"
he announced. "Each of you can take along fifty kilos of
belongings. Be ready on time, or you will be shot!"

Deportation? What did that mean?

Each of us gathered our best clothes. Dresses. Skirts. Sweaters. Coats. Shoes. Anything and everything we could think of—but only the best, for none of us knew how long the clothing would have to last.

I took my beautiful camel's-hair coat, which was too warm to wear at the end of May, but I couldn't leave it behind. I carried it under my arm, together with other precious clothing.

Lastly, we packed whatever food we had for our journey, just in case—just in case no one would feed us. It wasn't much, but there was bread, jam, and boiled potatoes.

In the dark hour of 4:00 A.M., May 29, 1944, hundreds of families throughout the ghetto began appearing in their courtyards. Each man, woman, and child was carrying a bundle, package, backpack, or suitcase. Each was taking along the best possessions of a lifetime.

A feeling of terror was in the air. There were Nazis with guns and dogs, watching our every move.

Somehow, my brother, Philip, disappeared.

"Thank God he escaped," my mother whispered.

But moments later, Philip was back. "I couldn't leave without you. We must all go together," he said.

We were herded to the railroad station—our family and all the other Jewish families of Kisvarda.

Main Street was lined with people—our Gentile neighbors. Many of our classmates were there, watching as the Nazis herded us past them. Some of the people were smiling. They seemed to know they would never see us again.

At the station, I wondered why the train had no passenger coaches, only cattle cars without windows. The answer was not long in coming. The Nazis began to force us into the cattle cars.

The Nazis shouted at us in German, a language we did not understand. It sounded like *Los! Los! Los!* It sounded like dogs barking.

They packed seventy-five to eighty people in each cattle car. Old men and women. Children clinging to their mothers. Infants in their mothers' arms.

Mama held Potyó close to her body. Philip piled our belongings around them as a wall of protection. Cipi, Chicha, Regina, and I held hands to keep from being separated. When the cattle car was stuffed to its limit, the door was sealed.

There were so many people and so little space, no one was able to sit. We could hardly breathe. With a squeal and a rumble, the train began to roll away from Kisvarda.

For two days, we were given no food to eat, no water to drink. We ate only what we had brought for the journey—the bread, jam, and boiled potatoes. The food was not enough, but we made it last by nibbling.

Many people fell ill. Mrs. Klein went crazy. She screamed hour after hour. Mrs. Fried's little girl, Sarah, died in her arms. Mrs. Hirsch's aged father died shortly after our journey began. But the train did not stop. When it did, on May thirty-first, we were in Poland, at a place called Auschwitz, a place none of us had ever heard of.

When the cattle car doors were opened, more Nazis with guns and dogs waited for us. Strange-looking men shouted us out of the train. All personal belongings were left behind. My beautiful camel's-hair coat, which I had guarded so carefully, was left on the cattle car floor.

"Out! Out! *Los! Los!* Fast! Fast!"

The shouting men were dressed in dirty striped suits, and they carried clubs. They beat anyone who moved too slowly. Later, we found out that they, too, were prisoners of the Nazis. Some were criminals who were working for the Germans.

"Stay with me! Stay together!" Mama shouted at us.

A handsome German officer with a silver pistol was in charge. He wore white gloves, and kept pointing his right thumb either to the left or to the right as each person passed before him. This inspection, we learned, was called "selection." The German officer was Dr. Josef Mengele.

Dr. Mengele sent Mama and my sister Potyó to the left.

"Be strong," Mama cried as she left us. "I love you."

Dr. Mengele sent the rest of us to the right.

"Potyó, I love you!" I shouted, but I don't know whether she heard me.

Philip was led away with the other men who had been sent to the right.

Cipi, Chicha, Regina, and I were taken with the other women to a large, wet room. There, in front of laughing German soldiers, we were forced to take off our clothes for what they called "disinfection."

Standing naked, we were embarrassed, ashamed, and frightened. Then, while we stood there, some women with clippers began to cut off all our hair. Regina and I were crying. Cipi and Chicha were sobbing and trying to hide their nakedness. But the Germans didn't care.

Soon we were totally without hair.

I stared at my sisters. They stared at me. I could hardly recognize them. They no longer looked like Cipi, Chicha, or Regina. They looked like strange two-legged animals that I had never seen before. I was sure that I looked the same to them.

A woman prisoner now threw ragged dresses at us, and we covered ourselves.

Suddenly, amid all the confusion and unseen by the Nazis, a young man without hair climbed through the window. "It's me, Philip," he whispered. "Eat whatever they give you, because we must survive. We are prisoners now in Auschwitz, but one day we will be free. And we will pay them back. So eat and survive. I love you."

Then he disappeared as swiftly and mysteriously as he had come.

from

Maus II: A Survivor's Tale

by Art Spiegelman

Spiegelman takes the comic book to a new level of seriousness, portraying Jews as mice, Poles as pigs, and Nazis as cats in two books of grim autobiography: *Maus: A Survivor's Tale*. The first book is subtitled *My Father Bleeds History*; the second, *And Here My Troubles Began*. Spiegelman won the Pulitzer Prize for *Maus*.

In these two episodes he asks his father, a Holocaust survivor, what happened in Auschwitz.

AUSCHWITZ WAS IN A TOWN CALLED OSWIECIM. BEFORE THE WAR I CAME OFTEN HERE TO SELL MY TEXTILES.

...AND NOW, I CAME AGAIN.

WE CAME TO A BIG HALL AND THEY SHOUTED ON US.

GET UNDRESSED! LEAVE YOUR VALUABLES! LINE UP! SCHNELL!

I WAS, AT THAT TIME, STILL WITH MY FRIEND MANDELBAUM.

THEY TOOK FROM US OUR PAPERS, OUR CLOTHES AND OUR HAIR..

(PSST- WH-WHAT'S GOING TO HAPPEN TO US?)

(DON'T WORRY..)

WE WERE COLD, AND WE WERE AFRAID.

(IF THEY BROUGHT YOU HERE, THEY'LL PUT YOU TO WORK. THEY'RE NOT READY TO KILL YOU YET.)

(WHAT ABOUT OUR WIVES AND OUR-)

SHUT UP, YIDS! TO THE BATH HOUSE. QUICK!

EVERYWHERE WE HAD TO RUN—SO LIKE *JOGGERS*— AND THEY RAN US TO THE SAUNA...

IN THE SNOW THEY THREW TO US PRISONERS CLOTHINGS.

ONE GUY TRIED TO EXCHANGE.

ALL AROUND WAS A SMELL SO TERRIBLE, I CAN'T EXPLAIN... SWEETISH... SO LIKE RUBBER BURNING. AND *FAT*.

HERE WAS ABRAHAM — MANDELBAUM'S NEPHEW!

UNCLE! UNCLE!

WHEN WE CAME INSIDE THE GATES SOMEONE RAN TO US FROM FAR AWAY.

SO, UNCLE... YOU'VE ENDED UP HERE TOO.

YOU *TOLD* US TO COME!

YOU WROTE US ABOUT HOW *HAPPY* YOU ARE IN HUNGARY—THAT WE SHOULD JOIN YOU RIGHT AWAY! WELL... HERE WE ARE.

HUNGARY. HAH!

THE POLES WHO ARRANGED OUR "ESCAPE" UNDERSTOOD *YIDDISH*. SO THEY KNEW YOU WERE WAITING TO HEAR IF I WAS SAFE.

IN BIELSKO THE POLES DICTATED THAT LETTER WHILE THE GESTAPO HELD A PISTOL UP TO MY HEAD.

WHAT COULD I DO? THEY'D HAVE SHOT ME THEN AND THERE.

WELL... SO HERE'S OUR HUNGARY...

AND THERE'S ONLY ONE WAY OUT OF HERE FOR ALL OF US ...THROUGH THOSE CHIMNEYS.

ABRAHAM I DIDN'T SEE AGAIN.... I THINK HE CAME OUT THE CHIMNEY.

BUT I SAW AGAIN ONCE THE POLES WHO BETRAYED US.

THE GERMANS DIDN'T NEED THEM. SO THEY FINISHED ALSO IN AUSCHWITZ.

WE NEWCOMERS WERE PUT INSIDE A ROOM. OLD-TIMERS PASSED AND SAID ALL THE SAME.

YOU SEE THOSE CHIMNEYS? ...

OKAY. SO I WAS **MORE** SAD.

I WAS WORN AND SHIVERING AND CRYING A LITTLE.

NOBODY EVEN **LOOKED**

BUT FROM ANOTHER ROOM SOMEONE APPROACHED OVER

WHY ARE YOU CRYING, MY SON?

SHOULD I BE **HAPPY**? AM I AT A CARNIVAL?

LET ME SEE YOUR ARM...

HE WAS A PRIEST...

HMM... YOUR NUMBER STARTS WITH 17. IN HEBREW THAT'S "K'MINYAN TOV." SEVENTEEN IS A VERY GOOD OMEN...

HE WASN'T JEWISH - BUT VERY INTELLIGENT!

IT ENDS WITH 13, THE AGE A JEWISH BOY BECOMES A MAN...

AND **LOOK**! ADDED TOGETHER IT TOTALS 18. THAT'S "CHAI," THE HEBREW NUMBER OF LIFE.

I CAN'T KNOW IF I'LL SURVIVE THIS HELL, BUT I'M CERTAIN **YOU'LL** COME THROUGH ALL THIS ALIVE!

I STARTED TO BELIEVE. I TELL YOU, HE PUT ANOTHER LIFE IN ME.

AND WHENEVER IT WAS VERY BAD I LOOKED AND SAID: "YES, THE PRIEST WAS **RIGHT**! IT TOTALS EIGHTEEN.

WHEW. THAT GUY WAS A **SAINT**!

YES... I NEVER SAW HIM AGAIN.

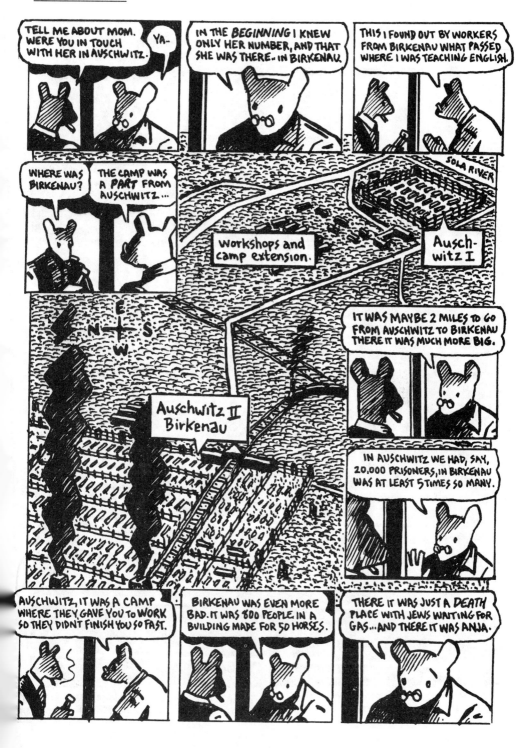

COME...IT'S TIME NOW WE'LL HURRY FOR LUNCH HOME TO THE BUNGALOW.

SO YOU WERE ACTUALLY IN *TOUCH* WITH ANJA IN BIRKENAU?

YAH. FROM MANCIE I HAD A REAL CONTACT WITH MOTHER, UNTIL LATER I COULD BRING ANJA TO—

WAIT! WHO'S MANCIE?

SHE WAS A HUNGARIAN, MANCIE, WHO WORKED SOMETIMES THERE. BEAUTIFUL. A TALL BLONDE GIRL. AND CLEVER.

(PSST, MISS—UP HERE! I SEE HOW KIND YOU ARE. HELP ME, PLEASE!)

HUH? (WHAT DO YOU WANT?)

REST BEHIND THAT STACK OF WOOD. I'LL WARN YOU IF A GUARD COMES CLOSE.

SHE HAD A LOVER, I HEARD LATER, AN S.S. MAN. HE GOT FOR HER A GOOD POSITION OVER 10 OR 12 OTHER GIRLS FROM BIRKENAU.

(NOTHING FOR ME, BUT I'M AFRAID FOR MY WIFE IN BIRKENAU. CAN YOU FIND OUT IF SHE'S STILL ALIVE?)

I TOLD TO HER ANJA'S NAME AND NUMBER.

(I'VE SAVED SOME FOOD. I CAN PAY FOR YOUR HELP.)

(KEEP YOUR FOOD. WE'LL BE WORKING HERE AGAIN IN A FEW DAYS. I'LL SEE WHAT I CAN FIND OUT.)

EACH DAY I LOOKED. FOUR DAYS AFTER, I SAW HER.

I MET A WOMAN NAMED ANJA FROM SOSNOWIEC. SHE'S VERY FRAIL...

SHE SPOKE OVER TO ONE OF HER WORKERS; I SPOKE ONLY TO MY TIN SO NOBODY WILL NOTICE.

SOMEONE TOLD HER THAT HER HUSBAND IS STILL ALIVE AND SHE STARTED SOBBING WITH JOY.

I HEARD THIS, AND I STARTED ALSO CRYING A LITTLE. AND MANCIE, SHE TOO STARTED CRYING.

A FEW DAYS AFTER, MANCIE AGAIN CAME THERE.

I PUT SOME "GARBAGE" UNDER A ROCK NEAR THE DOORWAY.

SHE BROUGHT TO ME A LETTER – A REAL LETTER! – FROM ANJA.

"I MISS YOU," SHE WROTE TO ME. "EACH DAY I THINK TO RUN INTO THE ELECTRIC WIRES AND FINISH EVERYTHING, BUT TO KNOW YOU ARE ALIVE IT GIVES ME STILL TO HOPE..."

SHE TOLD ME HER KAPO WAS VERY MEAN ON HER AND GAVE WORK ANJA REALLY COULDN'T DO.

LIKE TO RUN FROM THE KITCHEN WITH THE BIG CANS OF SOUP.

EVEN FOR ME SUCH CANS WERE HEAVY, AND FOR ANJA – SHE WAS SO SMALL – IT WAS IMPOSSIBLE,

SHE COULDN'T HOLD WELL HER END. ALWAYS SHE SPILLED.

THE KAPO BEAT ANJA VERY HARD BUT KEPT HER TO THIS JOB.

AND IF ANJA SPILLED OVER ALL FROM THE SOUP, THEN NOBODY GOT WHAT TO EAT, ESPECIALLY ANJA.

I WROTE TO HER. "I THINK OF YOU ALWAYS," AND SENT WITH MANCIE TWO PIECES OF BREAD.

IF THE S.S. WOULD SEE SHE IS TAKING FOOD INTO THE CAMP, RIGHT AWAY THEY WILL KILL HER. BUT ALWAYS SHE TOOK.

SO SHE SAID. "IF A COUPLE IS LOVING EACH OTHER SO MUCH, I MUST HELP HOWEVER I CAN."

from

Survival in Auschwitz

by Primo Levi

Primo Levi was a chemist whose anti-Fascist activities led to his arrest. He was deported to Auschwitz with other Italian Jews. Translated from the Italian by Stuart Woolf, these excerpts from Levi's personal account describe what happened to him and what he saw in the transports and the camps. The episode about Lorenzo dramatizes the role of the Righteous Gentile and shows how one person gave Levi a reason to live.

from On the Bottom

The journey did not last more than twenty minutes. Then the lorry stopped, and we saw a large door, and above it a sign, brightly illuminated (its memory still strikes me in my dreams): ARBEIT MACHT FREI, work gives freedom.*

We climb down, they make us enter an enormous empty room that is poorly heated. We have a terrible thirst. The weak gurgle of the water in the radiators makes us ferocious; we have had nothing to drink for four days. But there is also a tap—and above it a card which says that it is forbidden to drink as the water is dirty. Nonsense. It seems obvious that the card is a joke, "they" know that we are dying of thirst and they put us in a room, and there is a tap, and WASSERTRINKEN VERBOTEN.** I drink and I incite my companions to do likewise, but I have to spit it out, the water is tepid and sweetish, with the smell of a swamp.

This is hell. Today, in our times, hell must be like this. A huge, empty room: We are tired, standing on our feet, with a tap which drips while we cannot drink the water, and we wait for something which will certainly be terrible, and nothing happens and nothing continues to happen. What can one think about? One cannot think anymore, it is like being already dead. Someone sits down on the ground. The time passes drop by drop.

*Or, more exactly, "Work makes one free."
**"Drinking (of) water (is) forbidden."

We are not dead. The door is opened and an SS man enters, smoking. He looks at us slowly and asks, *"Wer kann Deutsch?"** One of us whom I have never seen, named Flesch, moves forward; he will be our interpreter. The SS man makes a long calm speech; the interpreter translates. We have to form rows of five, with intervals of two yards between man and man; then we have to undress and make a bundle of the clothes in a special manner, the woolen garments on one side, all the rest on the other; we must take off our shoes but pay great attention that they are not stolen.

Stolen by whom? Why should our shoes be stolen? And what about our documents, the few things we have in our pockets, our watches? We all look at the interpreter, and the interpreter asks the German, and the German smokes and looks him through and through as if he were transparent, as if no one had spoken.

I had never seen old men naked. Mr. Bergmann wore a truss and asked the interpreter if he should take it off, and the interpreter hesitated. But the German understood and spoke seriously to the interpreter, pointing to someone. We saw the interpreter swallow and then he said: "The officer says, take off the truss, and you will be given that of Mr. Coen." One could see the words coming bitterly out of Flesch's mouth; this was the German manner of laughing.

Now another German comes and tells us to put the shoes in a certain corner, and we put them there, because now it is all over and we feel outside this world and the only thing is to obey. Someone comes with a broom and sweeps

*"Who knows German?"

50

away all the shoes, outside the door in a heap. He is crazy, he is mixing them all together, ninety-six pairs, they will be all unmatched. The outside door opens, a freezing wind enters and we are naked and cover ourselves up with our arms. The wind blows and slams the door; the German reopens it and stands watching with interest how we writhe to hide from the wind, one behind the other. Then he leaves and closes it.

Now the second act begins. Four men with razors, soap-brushes, and clippers burst in; they have trousers and jackets with stripes, with a number sewn on the front; perhaps they are the same sort as those others of this evening (this evening or yesterday evening?); but these are robust and flourishing. We ask many questions but they catch hold of us and in a moment we find ourselves shaved and sheared. What comic faces we have without hair! The four speak a language which does not seem of this world. It is certainly not German, for I understand a little German.

Finally another door is opened: Here we are, locked in, naked, sheared and standing, with our feet in water—it is a shower room. We are alone. Slowly the astonishment dissolves, and we speak, and everyone asks questions and no one answers. If we are naked in a shower room, it means that we will have a shower. If we have a shower it is because they are not going to kill us yet. But why then do they keep us standing, and give us nothing to drink, while nobody explains anything, and we have no shoes or clothes, but we are all naked with our feet in the water, and we have been traveling five days and cannot even sit down.

And our women?

Mr. Levi asks me if I think that our women are like us at this moment, and where they are, and if we will be able to see them again. I say yes, because he is married and has a daughter; certainly we will see them again. But by now my belief is that all this is a game to mock and sneer at us. Clearly they will kill us, whoever thinks he is going to live is mad, it means that he has swallowed the bait, but I have not; I have understood that it will soon all be over, perhaps in this same room, when they get bored of seeing us naked, dancing from foot to foot and trying every now and again to sit down on the floor. But there are two inches of cold water and we cannot sit down.

We walk up and down without sense, and we talk, everybody talks to everybody else, we make a great noise. The door opens, and a German enters; it is the officer of before. He speaks briefly, the interpreter translates. "The officer says you must be quiet, because this is not a rabbinical school." One sees the words which are not his, the bad words, twist his mouth as they come out, as if he was spitting out a foul taste. We beg him to ask what we are waiting for, how long we will stay here, about our women, everything; but he says no, that he does not want to ask. This Flesch, who is most unwilling to translate into Italian the hard cold German phrases and refuses to turn into German our questions because he knows that it is useless, is a German Jew of about fifty, who has a large scar on his face from a wound received fighting the Italians on the Piave. He is a closed, taciturn man, for whom I feel an instinctive respect as I feel that he has begun to suffer before us.

The German goes and we remain silent, although we are a little ashamed of our silence. It is still night and we wonder if the day will ever come. The door opens again, and someone else dressed in stripes comes in. He is different from the others, older, with glasses, a more civilized face, and much less robust. He speaks to us in Italian.

By now we are tired of being amazed. We seem to be watching some mad play, one of those plays in which the witches, the Holy Spirit, and the devil appear. He speaks Italian badly, with a strong foreign accent. He makes a long speech, is very polite, and tries to reply to all our questions.

We are at Monowitz, near Auschwitz, in Upper Silesia, a region inhabited by both Poles and Germans. This camp is a work camp (in German one says *Arbeitslager*); all the prisoners (there are about ten thousand) work in a factory which produces a type of rubber called Buna, so that the camp itself is called Buna.

We will be given shoes and clothes—no, not our own—other shoes, other clothes, like his. We are naked now because we are waiting for the shower and the disinfection, which will take place immediately after the reveille, because one cannot enter the camp without being disinfected.

Certainly there will be work to do, everyone must work there. But there is work and work: He, for example, acts as doctor. He is a Hungarian doctor who studied in Italy and he is the dentist of the lager. He has been in the lager for four and a half years (not in this one: Buna has only been open for a year and a half), but we can see that he is still quite well, not very thin. Why is he in the lager? Is he Jewish like us? "No," he says simply, "I am a criminal."

We ask him many questions. He laughs, replies to some and not to others, and it is clear that he avoids certain subjects. He does not speak of the women: He says they are well, that we will see them again soon, but he does not say how or where. Instead he tells us other things, strange and crazy things; perhaps he too is playing with us. Perhaps he is mad—one goes mad in the lager. He says that every Sunday there are concerts and football matches. He says that whoever boxes well can become cook. He says that whoever works well receives prize coupons with which to buy tobacco and soap. He says that the water is really not drinkable, and that instead a coffee substitute is distributed every day, but generally nobody drinks it as the soup itself is sufficiently watery to quench thirst. We beg him to find us something to drink, but he says he cannot, that he has come to see us secretly, against SS orders, as we still have to be disinfected, and that he must leave at once; he has come because he has a liking for Italians, and because, he says, he "has a little heart." We ask him if there are other Italians in the camp and he says there are some, a few, he does not know how many; and he at once changes the subject. Meanwhile a bell rang and he immediately hurried off and left us stunned and disconcerted. Some feel refreshed but I do not. I still think that even this dentist, this incomprehensible person, wanted to amuse himself at our expense, and I do not want to believe a word of what he said.

At the sound of the bell, we can hear the still dark camp waking up. Unexpectedly the water gushes out boiling from the showers—five minutes of bliss; but immediately after, four men (perhaps they are the barbers) burst in yelling and shoving and drive us out, wet and steaming, into the adjoining room, which is freezing; here other shouting people throw at us unrecognizable rags and thrust into our hands a pair of broken down boots with wooden soles; we have no time to understand and we already find ourselves in the open, in the blue and icy snow of dawn, barefoot and naked, with all our clothing in our hands, with a hundred yards to run to the next hut. There we are finally allowed to get dressed.

When we finish, everyone remains in his own corner and we do not dare lift our eyes to look at one another. There is nowhere to look in a mirror, but our appearance stands in front of us, reflected in a hundred livid faces, in a hundred miserable and sordid puppets. We are transformed into the phantoms glimpsed yesterday evening.

Then for the first time we became aware that our language lacks words to express this offense, the demolition of a man. In a moment, with almost prophetic intuition, the reality was revealed to us: We had reached the bottom. It is not possible to sink lower than this; no human condition is more miserable than this, nor could it conceivably be so. Nothing belongs to us anymore; they have taken away our clothes, our shoes, even our hair; if we speak, they will not listen to us, and if they listen, they will not understand. They will even take away our name: and if we want to keep it, we will have to find ourselves the strength to do so, to manage somehow so that behind the name something of us, of us as we were, still remains.

We know that we will have difficulty in being understood, and this is as it should be. But consider what value, what meaning is enclosed even in the smallest of our daily habits, in the hundred possessions which even the poorest beggar owns: a handkerchief, an old letter, the photo of a cherished person. These things are part of us, almost like limbs of our body; nor is it conceivable that we can be deprived of them in our world, for we immediately find others to substitute [for] the old ones, other objects which are ours in their personification and evocation of our memories.

Imagine now a man who is deprived of everyone he loves,

and at the same time of his house, his habits, his clothes, in short, of everything he possesses: He will be a hollow man, reduced to suffering and needs, forgetful of dignity and restraint, for he who loses all often easily loses himself. He will be a man whose life or death can be lightly decided with no sense of human affinity, in the most fortunate of cases, on the basis of a pure judgment of utility. It is in this way that one can understand the double sense of the term "extermination camp" and it is now clear what we seek to express with the phrase "to lie on the bottom."

from The Events of the Summer

In this world shaken every day more deeply by the omens of its nearing end, amidst new terrors and hopes, with intervals of exasperated slavery, I happened to meet Lorenzo.

The story of my relationship with Lorenzo is both long and short, plain and enigmatic: It is the story of a time and condition now effaced from every present reality, and so I do not think it can be understood except in the manner in which we nowadays understand events of legends or the remotest history.

In concrete terms it amounts to little: An Italian civilian worker brought me a piece of bread and the remainder of his ration every day for six months; he gave me a vest of his, full of patches; he wrote a postcard on my behalf to Italy and brought me the reply. For all this he neither asked nor accepted any reward, because he was good and simple and did not think that one did good for a reward.

. . . We are the untouchables to the civilians. They think, more or less explicitly—with all the nuances lying between contempt and commiseration—that as we have been condemned to this life of ours, reduced to our condition, we must be tainted by some mysterious, grave sin. They hear us speak in many different languages, which they do not understand and which sound to them as grotesque as animal noises; they see us reduced to ignoble slavery, without hair, without honor and without names, beaten every day, more abject every day, and they never see in our eyes a light of rebellion, or of peace, or of faith. They know us as thieves and untrustworthy, muddy, ragged and starving, and mistaking the effect for the cause, they judge us worthy of our abasement. Who could tell one of our faces from the other? For them we are *"Kazett,"* a singular neuter word.

This naturally does not stop many of them throwing us a piece of bread or a potato now and again, or giving us their bowls, after the distribution of *"Zivilsuppe"* in the workyards, to scrape and give back washed. They do it to get rid of some importunate starved look, or through a momentary impulse of humanity, or through simple curiosity to see us running from all sides to fight each other for the scrap, bestially and without restraint, until the strongest one gobbles it up, whereupon all the others limp away, frustrated.

Now nothing of this sort occurred between me and Lorenzo. However little sense there may be in trying to specify why I, rather than thousands of others, managed to survive the test, I believe that it was really due to Lorenzo that I am alive today; and not so much for his material aid, as for his having constantly reminded me by his presence, by his natural and plain manner of being good, that there still existed a just world outside our own, something and someone still pure and whole, not corrupt, not savage, extraneous to hatred and terror; something difficult to define, a remote possibility of good, but for which it was worth surviving.

The personages in these pages are not men. Their humanity is buried, or they themselves have buried it, under an offense received or inflicted on someone else. The evil and insane SS men, the kapos, the politicals, the criminals, the prominents, great and small, down to the indifferent slave Häftlinge, all the grades of the mad hierarchy created by the Germans paradoxically fraternized in a uniform internal desolation.

But Lorenzo was a man; his humanity was pure and uncontaminated, he was outside this world of negation. Thanks to Lorenzo, I managed not to forget that I myself was a man.

The Shawl

by Cynthia Ozick

"The Shawl" was awarded first prize in the O. Henry Prize Stories in 1981 and was included in *Best American Short Stories* of that year.

Stella, cold, cold, the coldness of hell. How they walked on the roads together, Rosa with Magda curled up between sore breasts, Magda wound up in the shawl. Sometimes Stella carried Magda. But she was jealous of Magda. A thin girl of fourteen, too small, with thin breasts of her own, Stella wanted to be wrapped in a shawl, hidden away, asleep, rocked by the march, a baby, a round infant in arms. Magda took Rosa's nipple, and Rosa never stopped walking, a walking cradle. There was not enough milk; sometimes Magda sucked air; then she screamed. Stella was ravenous. Her knees were tumors on sticks, her elbows chicken bones.

Rosa did not feel hunger; she felt light, not like someone walking but like someone in a faint, in a trance, arrested in a fit, someone who is already a floating angel, alert and seeing everything, but in the air, not there, not touching the road. As if teetering on the tips of her fingernails. She looked into Magda's face through a gap in the shawl: a squirrel in a nest, safe, no one could reach her inside the little house of the shawl's windings. The face, very round, a pocket mirror of a face: but it was not Rosa's bleak complexion, dark like cholera, it was another kind of face altogether, eyes blue as air, smooth feathers of hair nearly as yellow as the star sewn into Rosa's coat. You could think she was one of *their* babies.

Rosa, floating, dreamed of giving Magda away in one of the villages. She could leave the line for a minute and push Magda into the hands of any woman on the side of the road. But if she moved out of line they might shoot. And even if she fled the line for half a second and pushed the shawl-bundle at a stranger, would the woman take it? She might be surprised, or afraid; she might drop the shawl, and Magda would fall out and strike her head and die. The little round head. Such a good child, she gave up screaming, and sucked now only for the taste of the drying nipple itself. The neat grip of the tiny gums. One mite of a tooth tip sticking up in the bottom gum, how shining, an elfin tombstone of white marble gleaming there. Without complaining, Magda relinquished Rosa's teats, first the left, then the right; both were cracked, not a sniff of milk. The duct-crevice extinct, a dead volcano, blind eye, chill hole, so Magda took the corner of the shawl and milked it instead. She sucked and sucked, flooding the threads with wetness. The shawl's good flavor, milk of linen.

It was a magic shawl, it could nourish an infant for three days and three nights. Magda did not die, she stayed alive, although very quiet. A peculiar smell, of cinnamon and almonds, lifted out of her mouth. She held her eyes open every moment, forgetting how to blink or nap, and Rosa and sometimes Stella studied their blueness. On the road they raised one burden of a leg after another and studied Magda's face. "Aryan," Stella said, in a voice grown as thin as a string; and Rosa thought how Stella gazed at Magda like a young cannibal. And the time that Stella said "Aryan," it sounded to Rosa as if Stella had really said "Let us devour her."

But Magda lived to walk. She lived that long, but she did not walk very well, partly because she was only fifteen months old, and partly because the spindles of her legs could not hold up her fat belly. It was fat with air, full and round. Rosa gave almost all her food to Magda, Stella gave nothing; Stella was ravenous, a growing child herself, but not growing much. Stella did not menstruate. Rosa did not menstruate. Rosa was ravenous, but also not; she learned from Magda how to drink the taste of a finger in one's mouth. They were in a place without pity, all pity was annihilated in Rosa, she looked at Stella's bones without pity. She was sure that Stella was waiting for Magda to die so she could put her teeth into the little thighs.

Rosa knew Magda was going to die very soon; she should have been dead already, but she had been buried away deep inside the magic shawl, mistaken there for the shivering mound of Rosa's breasts; Rosa clung to the shawl as if it covered only herself. No one took it away from her. Magda was mute. She never cried. Rosa hid her in the barracks, under the shawl, but she knew that one day someone would inform; or one day someone, not even Stella, would steal Magda to eat her. When Magda began to walk, Rosa knew that Magda was going to die very soon, something would happen. She was afraid to fall asleep; she slept with the weight of her thigh on Magda's body; she was afraid she would smother Magda under her thigh. The weight of Rosa was becoming less and less; Rosa and Stella were slowly turning into air.

Magda was quiet, but her eyes were horribly alive, like blue tigers. She watched. Sometimes she laughed—it seemed a laugh, but how could it be? Magda had never seen anyone laugh. Still, Magda laughed at her shawl when the wind blew its corners, the bad wind with pieces of black in it, that made Stella's and Rosa's eyes tear. Magda's eyes were always clear and tearless. She watched like a tiger. She guarded her shawl. No one could touch it; only Rosa could touch it. Stella was not allowed. The shawl was Magda's own baby, her pet, her little sister. She tangled herself up in it and sucked on one of the corners when she wanted to be very still.

Then Stella took the shawl away and made Magda die.

Afterward Stella said: "I was cold."

And afterward she was always cold, always. The cold went into her heart: Rosa saw that Stella's heart was cold. Magda flopped onward with her little pencil legs scribbling this way and that, in search of the shawl; the pencils faltered at the barracks opening, where the light began. Rosa saw and pursued. But already Magda was in the square outside the barracks, in the jolly light. It was the roll-call arena. Every morning Rosa had to conceal Magda under the shawl against a wall of the barracks and go out and stand in the arena with Stella and hundreds of others, sometimes for hours, and Magda, deserted, was quiet under the shawl, sucking on her corner. Every day Magda was silent, and so she did not die. Rosa saw that today Magda was going to die, and at the same time a fearful joy ran in Rosa's two palms, her fingers were on fire, she was astonished, febrile: Magda, in the sunlight, swaying on her pencil legs, was howling. Ever since the drying up of Rosa's nipples, ever since Magda's last scream on the road, Magda had been devoid of any syllable; Magda was a mute. Rosa believed that something had gone wrong with her vocal cords, with her windpipe, with the cave of her larynx; Magda was defective, without a voice; perhaps she was deaf; there might be something amiss with her intelligence; Magda was dumb. Even the laugh that came when the ash-stippled wind made a clown out of Magda's shawl was only the airblown showing of her teeth. Even when the lice, head lice and body lice, crazed her so that she became as wild as one of the big rats that plundered the barracks at daybreak looking for carrion, she rubbed and scratched and kicked and bit and rolled without a whimper. But now Magda's mouth was spilling a long viscous rope of clamor.

"Maaaa—"

It was the first noise Magda had ever sent out from her throat since the drying up of Rosa's nipples.

"Maaaa . . . aaa!"

Again! Magda was wavering in the perilous sunlight of the arena, scribbling on such pitiful little bent shins. Rosa saw. She saw that Magda was grieving for the loss of her shawl, she saw that Magda was going to die. A tide of commands hammered in Rosa's nipples: Fetch, get, bring! But she did not know which to go after first, Magda or the shawl. If she jumped out into the arena to snatch Magda up, the howling would not stop, because Magda would still not have the shawl; but if she ran back into the barracks to find the shawl, and if she found it, and if she came after Magda holding it and shaking it, then she would get Magda back, Magda would put the shawl in her mouth and turn dumb again.

Rosa entered the dark. It was easy to discover the shawl. Stella was heaped under it, asleep in her thin bones. Rosa tore the shawl free and flew—she could fly, she was only air—into the arena. The sunheat murmured of another life, of butterflies in summer. The light was placid, mellow. On the other side of the steel fence, far away, there were green meadows speckled with dandelions and deep-colored violets; beyond them, even farther, innocent tiger lilies, tall, lifting their orange bonnets. In the barracks they spoke of "flowers," of "rain": excrement, thick turd-braids, and the slow stinking maroon waterfall that slunk down from the upper bunks, the stink mixed with a bitter fatty floating smoke that greased Rosa's skin. She stood for an instant at the margin of the arena. Sometimes the electricity inside the fence would seem to hum; even Stella said it was only an imagining, but Rosa heard real sounds in the wire: grainy sad voices. The farther she was from the fence, the more clearly the voices crowded at her. The lamenting voices strummed so convincingly, so passionately, it was impossible to suspect them of being phantoms. The voices told her to hold up the shawl, high; the voices told her to shake it, to whip with it, to unfurl it like a flag. Rosa lifted, shook, whipped, unfurled. Far off, very far, Magda leaned across her air-fed belly, reaching out with the rods of her arms. She was high up, elevated, riding someone's shoulder. But the shoulder that carried Magda was not coming toward Rosa and the shawl, it was drifting away, the speck of Magda was moving more and more into the smoky distance. Above the shoulder a helmet glinted. The light tapped the helmet and sparkled it into a goblet. Below the helmet a black body like a domino and a pair of black boots hurled themselves in the direction of the electrified fence. The electric voices began to chatter wildly. "Maamaa, maaamaaa," they all hummed together. How far Magda was from Rosa now, across the whole square, past a dozen barracks, all the way on the other side! She was no bigger than a moth.

All at once Magda was swimming through the air. The whole of Magda traveled through loftiness. She looked like a butterfly touching a silver vine. And the moment Magda's feathered round head and her pencil legs and balloonish belly and zigzag arms splashed against the fence, the steel voices went mad in their growling, urging Rosa to run and run to the spot where Magda had fallen from her flight against the electrified fence; but of course Rosa did not obey them. She only stood, because if she ran they would shoot, and if she tried to pick up the sticks of Magda's body they would shoot, and if she let the wolf's screech ascending now through the ladder of her skeleton break out, they would shoot; so she took Magda's shawl and filled her own mouth with it, stuffed it in and stuffed it in, until she was swallowing up the wolf's screech and tasting the cinnamon and almond depth of Magda's saliva; and Rosa drank Magda's shawl until it dried.

Shoah: An Oral History of the Holocaust

by Claude Lanzmann

In Lanzmann's nine-and-a-half-hour film, survivors tell what happened and so do the bureaucrats and engineers who made the machinery of death possible.

The complete text of the film was published as a book in 1985. Here are three of the many interviews that make up Lanzmann's masterpiece. ABRAHAM BOMBA, a barber who survived Treblinka, is haunted by how a whole world can be exterminated in a moment. FRANZ SUCHOMEL, one of the SS officers at the smooth-running camp Treblinka, denies knowing it was a death camp. RAUL HILBERG, a historian, discusses what the Nazis got from the past.

Shoah is Hebrew for Holocaust.

Abraham Bomba

At that time we started working in that place they called Treblinka. Still I couldn't believe what had happened over there on the other side of the gate, where the people went in, everything disappeared, and everything got quiet. But in a minute we find out, when we start to ask the people who worked here before us what had happened to the others, they said, "What do you mean, what happened? Don't you know that? They're all gassed, all killed." It was impossible to say anything—we were just like stones. We couldn't ask what had happened to the wife, to the kid. "What do you mean—wife, kid? Nobody is anymore!" How could they kill, how could they gas so many people at once? But they had a way to do it.

That's how the day went through, without anything. Not drinking—we went twenty-four hours without water, without anything. We couldn't drink—we couldn't take anything into our mouths, because it was impossible to believe that just a minute, just an hour before, you were part of a family, you were part of a wife or a husband, and now all of a sudden everything is dead.

We went into a special barrack, where I was sleeping right next to the hallway. And over there, that night was the most horrible night for all the people, because of the memory of all those things that people went through with each other—all the joys and the happiness and the births and the weddings and other things—and all of a sudden, in one second, to cut through without anything, and without any guilt of the people, because the people weren't guilty at all. The only guilt they had was that they were Jewish.

Most of us were up all night, trying to talk to each other, which was not allowed. The kapo that was sleeping in the same barrack . . . we were not allowed to talk to each other or to express our views or our minds to each other. And till the morning at five o'clock we start going out from the barrack. In the morning when they had the appeal to go out from the barracks, from our group I would say at least four or five were dead. I don't know how that happened—they must have had with them some kind of poison and poisoned themselves. At least two of them were my close friends. They didn't say anything. We didn't even know they had poison with them.

Franz Suchomel, SS Unterscharführer

What was Treblinka like then?

Treblinka then was operating at full capacity.

Full capacity?

Full capacity! The Warsaw Ghetto was being emptied then. Three trains arrived in two days, each with three, four, five thousand people aboard, all from Warsaw. But at the same time, other trains came in from Kielce and other places. So three trains arrived, and since the offensive against Stalingrad was in full swing, the trainloads of Jews were left on a station siding. What's more, the cars were French, made of steel. So that while five thousand Jews arrived in Treblinka, three thousand were dead in the cars. They had slashed their wrists, or just died. The ones we unloaded were half dead and half mad. In the other trains from Kielce and elsewhere, at least half were dead. We stacked them here, here, here, and here. Thousands of people piled one on top of another on the ramp. Stacked like wood. In addition, other Jews, still alive, waited there for two days: The small gas chambers could no longer handle the load. They functioned day and night in that period.

Can you please describe, very precisely, your first impression of Treblinka? Very precisely. It's very important.

My first impression of Treblinka, and that of some of the other men, was catastrophic. For we had not been told how and what . . . that people were being killed there. They hadn't told us.

You didn't know?

No!

Incredible!

But true. I didn't want to go. That was proved at my trial. I was told: "Mr. Suchomel, there are big workshops there for tailors and shoemakers, and you'll be guarding them."

But you knew it was a camp?

Yes. We were told: "The Führer ordered a *resettlement program. It's an order from the Führer.*" Understand?

Resettlement program.

Resettlement program. No one ever spoke of killing.

Raul Hilberg

What did they get from the past, the Nazis?

They got the actual content of measures which they took. For example, the barring of Jews from office, the prohibition of intermarriages and of the employment in Jewish homes of female persons under the age of forty-five, the various marking decrees—especially the Jewish star—the compulsory ghetto, the voidance of any will executed by a Jew that might work in such a way as to prevent inheritance of his property by someone who was a Christian. Many such measures had been worked out over the course of more than a thousand years by authorities of the church and by secular governments that followed in those footsteps. And the experience gathered over that time became a reservoir that could be used, and which indeed was used to an amazing extent. One can compare a rather large number of German laws with their counterparts in the past and find complete parallels, even in detail, as if there were a memory which automatically extended to the period of 1933, 1935, 1939, and beyond.

They invented very little, and they did not invent the portrait of the Jew, which also was taken over lock, stock, and barrel from writings going back to the sixteenth century. So even the propaganda, the realm of imagination and invention—even there they were remarkably in the footsteps of those who preceded them, from Martin Luther to the nineteenth century. And here again they were not inventive.

They had to become inventive with the "final solution." That was their great invention, and that is what made this entire process different from all others that had preceded that event. In this respect, what transpired when the "final solution" was adopted—or, to be more precise, bureaucracy moved into it—was a turning point in history. Even here I would suggest a logical progression, one that came to fruition in what might be called closure, because from the earliest days, from the fourth century, the sixth century, the missionaries of Christianity had said in effect to the Jews: "You may not live among us as Jews." The secular rulers who followed them from the late Middle Ages then decided: "You may not live among us," and the Nazis finally decreed: "You may not live." Conversion was followed by expulsion, and the third was the territorial solution, which was of course the solution carried out in the territories under German command, excluding emigration: death. The "final solution." And the "final solution," you see, is really final, because people who are converted can yet be Jews in secret, people who are expelled can yet return. But people who are dead will not reappear.

Nightfather

by Carl Friedman

Carl Friedman is a Dutch poet and
translator, and her father is a Holocaust
survivor. Translated from the Dutch by
Arnold and Erica Pomerans, her
autobiographical novel is made up of a
number of intense episodes about a
young girl in the Netherlands in the
1950s and 1960s who tells how her
father's stories of his life in the
concentration camps are part of family
life. Always she and her brothers, Max
and Simon, must listen to the stories of
the camps.

No End

"István was a Hungarian Gypsy, nicknamed Rudolph Valentino. He had jet-black eyebrows, more sharply defined than if they'd been painted on. We shared a bunk in a fraternal way, as well as a lot of fat lice that commuted between his rags and mine in a continuous stream of rush-hour traffic. He spoke in a lilting dialect, most of which I couldn't understand. Even the few words of German he had picked up from the SS sounded melodious in his mouth.

"Although he wasn't a member of the camp orchestra, he owned a fiddle, and would play many a czárdás for us in the evenings. The block leader loved to listen and would reward him with a piece of bread or some leftover soup, half of which István always passed on to me. If a violin string broke during one of his performances, he'd pull a handful of brand new ones out of his pocket, cool as a cucumber. He was amazing, he could steal an egg out of a hen's backside before she even knew she was going to lay.

"He could swipe the most outlandish things, from blue suede shoes to real caraway cheese. Once he even pinched a compass for us to use during our escape. Because escape we surely would, in a week or a month, no doubt, according to István. I would nod in agreement, but only half-heartedly. Escape was as good as impossible. Whoever tried it usually didn't get very far. The dogs would pick up his scent and when he was returned to the camp he'd be strung up. Sometimes, as a little joke, the SS would dump the fugitive's corpse onto a chair and hang a notice around his neck reading BACK AGAIN! I'd been a prisoner long enough to understand that the chances of survival on the other side of the barbed wire were not much greater than they were inside. István didn't know that, or didn't want to know. Every night he sat bent over the compass like a child, seeing in it not just the cardinal points but the whole wide world: forests, mountains, rivers. Even the stars and the planets were mirrored in his dark eyes.

"At the time, my *Arbeitskommando* had the job of unloading stones. It worked like this. One of the prisoners would stand on a truck and throw the stones at top speed to another prisoner standing below, who would catch them and pass them on to the next in line. The catcher at the bottom of the truck had the worst of it, and at night his hands were as raw as fresh steak. Willi Hammer, with his peculiar sense of humor, made me the catcher time after time, until every nerve in my fingers was exposed and small cauliflower-shaped swellings began growing from the bone.

"Other catchers got that too. Skozepa, a Czech, went to the hospital block with it. When he came back, he had no more swellings but no more fingers, either: They'd been cut off with a pair of rubber-cutters. Before he was gassed, we fed him bread with a finger-thick layer of beet-root jam on it, something nobody begrudged him.

"A few days later, a beaming István pushed a small bundle toward me that turned out to contain a tube of sulfur ointment, some clean rags, and a large safety pin. The safety pin was my salvation: I held it in the fire, tore my festering fingers open from top to bottom and dislodged the cauliflowers one by one."

My father places his hands palms up on the table. We know those thin scars pointing like arrows to the scar tissue on his fingertips, but we look all the same.

"István," he says, "István." He shakes his head slowly. "I don't know what got into him all of a sudden. He abandoned all hope of escaping. He stopped making music. Night after night he sat in a corner of the barracks staring in front of him. 'I can see no end to it,' he would say dejectedly, 'no end, no end.'

"He became reckless, would march out of step, and stole like a magpie. He wouldn't get up on his own in the mornings and had to be clubbed out of his bunk. One morning the inevitable happened.

"I can still remember as if it were yesterday. We were lined up, by blocks, on the snowy assembly ground, standing at attention and ready for inspection by the SS. As soon as the guards showed up, we were supposed to salute them by turning our heads in their direction and removing our caps. The problem was that they always approached from the rear, and we, standing there looking straight ahead, couldn't tell which side they were coming from. To keep mistakes to a minimum, the block leader, who *could* see them coming, had thought up a little ruse. If the SS came from the left he would give the order *'Caps off!'* If they came from the right, he would just shout *'Caps!'* This ploy saved us from a lot of beatings and punishment drill.

"On this particular morning, István was about six rows in front of me, standing rigidly in line like everybody else. We could hear the SS boots. *'Caps off!'* came the command.

In unison we looked over our left shoulders and bared our heads. Then there was an ominous silence. Thinking that some idiot had turned the wrong way, I glanced at the other rows out of the corner of my eye."

In the course of telling this story, my father has risen to his feet. He is standing stiffly at attention beside his chair, an invisible cap in his right hand. Slowly he raises this hand and points a finger at a spot in the room where we can see absolutely nothing. His face begins to glow.

"Just imagine," he says, "those rows of prisoners, shaven heads as far as the eye could see. And right in the middle there stood István with—and God alone knows where it had come from—a red tin toy car on the top of his bald head. The thing was held on with bits of string, violin strings probably, which ran from the little wheels down to István's chin, under which he had knotted the ends.

"It was the only time I was in the camp that I saw the SS speechless. Their surprise didn't last very long, of course, a moment at the most, but a moment during which a single *Untermensch*, just one 'subhuman,' made a laughingstock of the whole Third Reich while standing stiff as a ramrod, not moving a muscle, until they dragged him out of the lines.

"Barely half an hour later he was strung up on the gallows before a large audience. We were ordered to march close up to his tortured body and to look at it for two whole minutes. The SS had removed the little red car, as if they were afraid we might go on laughing."

Questions

"If God exists," says Max, "then why didn't he do anything?"

My father, who has finished eating, lights a cigarette.

"What do you mean?" he asks, blowing smoke out of his nostrils.

"He could have stopped the trains, couldn't he? He could have knocked the camp down with one finger, couldn't he? Why didn't he help you?"

"God isn't some kind of odd-job man." My father smiles. "Imagine if he were there to do our bidding the whole time. What a mess we'd be in then!"

"Aren't you angry with him?"

"Now and then."

"But you still believe in him?"

"You could call it that."

"I think that's stupid!" Max says piercingly. My father sighs.

"You can't blame God. God didn't shout *Sieg Heil!* when Adolf Hitler came to power. God didn't cheer when Europe was trampled underfoot. People like you and me did that. The trains were driven by human beings, the gas chambers were invented by human beings. Of course, those people had been created by God, but they had free will. They could do what they felt like, and it just so happened that they felt like genocide."

"If God created all men, then he created Hitler, too!" says Max triumphantly.

"That's undeniably so," my father replies calmly, "but Hitler was responsible for his own actions."

"And God just let him get away with it?" says Max, aggrieved. "But that's not fair!"

"No one says it's fair. If you want a fair world, you'll have to look for another one."

Max blinks.

"So you believe in some bastard of a God who looks on without raising an eyebrow while everyone's being killed?"

"There's no alternative," says my father. "I'd rather have a God I can't understand than no God at all. So I'll have to put up with him, for better or worse."

"Suit yourself!" cries Max. "Just don't keep coming to me with stories about that stupid camp of yours. It served you right!"

My father raises his finger, and shakes it threateningly over the dishes.

"I don't like your tone!"

"Oh, no? And what are you going to do about it?"

My mother gets up from the table.

"Be quiet, Max."

"Why don't you hit me then?" Max yells at my father. "Just like the SS!" My mother pulls him off his chair and starts pushing him toward the door. "Kick me to death, why don't you!" Max shouts over her shoulder. "Why don't you gas me!"

Simon is pinching my arm. He's doing his best not to burst into tears. My father gasps for air.

"Come now, Ephraim," says my mother. She lays her hand on his, but he shakes it off and rubs his face.

"What do you all want from me?" he says. "It's hard enough as it is."

Splinter

by Ida Fink

Ida Fink survived the war in hiding.
After the war she and her family settled
in Israel. Translated from the Polish by
Madeline Levine and Francine Prose, this
short story from *A Scrap of Time and
Other Stories* is about how Nazi terror
invaded ordinary homes. The collection
won the first Anne Frank Prize for
Literature.

In an interview in the *New York Times
Book Review* (July 12, 1987), Ida Fink
said, "I thought one should talk about
these things in a quiet voice."

The girl touched his arm with her hand, her delicate, manicured hand, blossoming with polished pink nails.

She said, "Let's not talk about that any more. You promised."

They were walking along a steep road in the hills of a defeated country, in a region unscathed by war, clean and radiant. The meadows with their lush, long, unmown grass looked especially lovely—bright with flowers and alive with the chirping of crickets. Summer had come unusually early this year. It was only the beginning of June and already the air was heavy with the smell of the lindens.

They were both very young and they were going on a picnic. When she asked him to stop talking, the boy fell silent in embarrassment. He smiled sheepishly and said, "Look, I've got to tell everything to the end. And since I don't have anyone but you . . . It's like a deep splinter that has to be removed so it won't fester. Do you understand?"

"I understand, I understand, only you can't talk about it all the time, without stopping. You haven't stopped for"—she hesitated; they had known each other scarcely a week—"*days*. It's for your sake that I want you to stop. But if you think it helps to . . ."

She raised her beautiful hands in a gesture of helplessness. She was giving in.

"It's beautiful here," said the boy. "This picnic was a good idea. Your idea. You always have the good ideas, I'm still not much good for anything."

"Don't worry. At first I used to think pretty clothes would never make me happy again." She laughed. She was wearing a bright print dress flowered like the meadow.

"You! You were lucky. You spent the whole time in the country, you fed chickens. Come on, don't get angry, that's really terrific luck, and that's why you're so lovely and calm and why I need you. You have such beautiful legs! I'd like to paint them someday. I always wanted to paint. Always, before the war, that is. But I was thirteen then."

The sun was setting when they entered the dense forest; the pine trees stood in rows like soldiers. The soft needles gave way beneath their feet.

"Speaking of good ideas," said the girl, "let's go to the movies tonight. Or to a dance. Okay?"

The boy bent down, picked up a pine cone, sniffed it. "Let's take a little rest," he said.

They lay down on their backs and looked up at the pure, pale blue sky suspended over the woods.

"My mother would be very happy," he began. His eyes were closed; his long lashes emphasized his pallor. He waited a moment, but the girl did not ask why. So he went on:

"She would have been very happy to know that I am lying here in the woods with a girl I love, that I'm lying around on such a splendidly happy day, with nothing threatening me. Because she was probably thinking of that when . . ."

Again he fell silent. The girl lay motionless with her hands under her head and gnawed on a blade of grass.

"What happened with my mother was the worst thing possible," he said after a moment. "Worse than the bunker in the forest where I ate leaves and roots for a week— remember I told you?—worse than a beating in the camp. You have hands just like my mother's. She was very beautiful. We were living in a small, dirty room. Father was already in the camp, and we had nothing to eat. But my mother was still beautiful and cheerful and never showed any fear in my presence. I was terribly afraid. She was, too, I knew it, her quiet crying would often wake me up at night, but I would lie still as a mouse so she could cry in private. Before what I am about to tell you happened, my mother was crying less often at night, because we were supposed to get papers and cross to the other side. Now *I* couldn't fall asleep, I was so worried about whether our papers would arrive in time. She was calm; she taught me different prayers and how to cross myself, and carols, because it was almost Christmas.

"I didn't sleep *that* night, either. I heard them come through the gate, but I was speechless with terror. I lay there stupefied, I couldn't even call out 'Mama.' I heard wailing from the ground floor; they were beating people. I didn't scream until they were walking up the stairs. Those stairs used to creak, I can still hear them creaking, it's funny, isn't it?"

He paused, listening intently. The wind was blowing and several pine cones fell from the tree. It was hot, as before a storm.

"How did she do it? It was unbelievable—it took her just a few seconds. Later I often thought that she must have rehearsed that moment beforehand, she acted so quickly and efficiently. She jumped out of bed, scooped up the bedding in one motion and stuffed it into the bureau drawer; in a second she had folded up her cot and slipped it behind the wardrobe. Then she grabbed my hand and shoved me into the corner by the door, and before they could pound on it, she opened it wide and hospitably. The heavy oak door pressed me against the wall and hid me. There was only one bed and one person in the room. I heard her ask in German, "What's the matter?" Her voice was so calm she could have been speaking to the mailman. They struck her in the face and ordered her, just as she was, in her nightgown, to go downstairs."

He took a deep breath. "That's almost all there is to say. Almost. . . . Because you know, when my mother pressed me against the wall with the door, I grabbed the handle and held on to it, even though it wouldn't have shut on its own, since it was a heavy door and the floor was uneven."

The boy fell silent; he brushed away a bee. Then he added, "I would give a great deal to let go of that handle . . . ," and then, with a smile that begged forgiveness, he added, "You'll have to have a lot of patience with me. All right?"

He turned over lazily and looked at her face. The girl was gorgeous, slightly pink. Her warm lips were parted, she was breathing calmly, evenly. She was asleep.

A Minority

by Frank O'Connor

In O'Connor's famous story, the
Holocaust reaches from Germany to an
Irish boarding school.

Denis Halligan noticed Willy Stein for the first time one
Sunday when the other fellows were at Mass. As Denis was
a Protestant, he didn't go to Mass. Instead, he sat on the
steps outside the chapel with Willy. Willy was a thin,
seedy little chap with long, wild hair. It was an autumn
morning; there was mist on the trees, and you could
scarcely see the great ring of mountains that cut them off
there in the middle of Ireland, miles from anywhere.

"Why did they send you here if you're a Proddy?" asked
Willy.

"I don't know," said Denis, who felt his background
was so queer that he didn't want to explain it to anybody.
"I suppose because it was cheap."

"Is your old fellow a Catholic?" asked Willy.

"No," replied Denis. "Is yours?"

"No," Willy said contemptuously. "He was a Proddy. My old one was a Proddy, too."

"Where do they live?" asked Denis.

"They're dead," Willy said, making the motion of spitting. "The bloody Germans killed them."

"Oh, cripes!" Denis said regretfully. Denis had a great admiration for everything German, particularly tank generals, and when he grew up he wanted to be a tank general himself, but it seemed a pity that they had to kill Willy's father and mother. Bad as it was to have your parents separated, as his own were, it was worse having them dead. "Was it a bomb?" he asked.

"No," Willy replied without undue emotion. "They were killed in a camp. They sent me over to the Cumminses in Dublin or I'd have been killed, too. The Cumminses are Catholics. That's why I was sent here."

"Do you like it here?" asked Denis.

"I do not," Willy said scornfully in his slummy Dublin accent, and then took out a slingshot and fitted a stone in it. "I'd sooner Vienna. Vienna was gas. When I grow up I'm going to get out of this blooming place."

"But what will you do?"

"Aw, go to sea or something. I don't care."

Denis was interested in Willy. Apart from the fact that they were the only Proddies in the school, Willy struck him as being really tough, and Denis admired toughness. He was always trying to be tough himself, but there was a soft streak in him that kept breaking out. It was breaking out now, and he knew it. Though he saw that Willy didn't give a rap about his parents, Denis couldn't help being sorry for him, alone in the middle of Ireland with his father and mother dead half a world away. He said as much to his friend Nigel Healy, from Cork, that afternoon, but Nigel only gave a superior sniff.

"But that fellow is mad," he said, in his reasonable way.

"How is he mad?" asked Denis.

"He's not even let go home on holidays," explained Nigel. "He has to stay here all during the summer. Those people were nice to him, and what does he do? Breaks every window in the place. They had the police to the house twice. He's mad on slingshots."

"He had one this morning," said Denis.

"Last time he was caught with one he got flogged," said Nigel. "You see, the fellow has no sense. I even saw him putting sugar on his meat."

"But why did he do that?" asked Denis.

"Said he liked it," replied Nigel with a smile and a shrug. "He's bound to get expelled one of these days. You'd want to mind yourself with him."

But for some reason that only made Denis more interested in Willy Stein, and he looked forward to meeting him again by himself the following Sunday. He was curious to know why the Germans would want to kill Stein's father and mother. That seemed to him a funny thing to do— unless, of course, they were spies for the English.

Again they sat on the steps, but this morning the sun was warm and bright, and the mountains all around them were a brilliant blue. If Stein's parents were really spies, the idea of it did not seem to have occurred to him. According to him, his father had been a lawyer and his mother something on a newspaper, and he didn't seem to remember much about them except that they were both "gas." Everything with Stein was "gas." His mother was gentle and timid, and let him have everything he wanted, so she was "great gas." His father was sure she was ruining him, and was always on to him to study and be better than other kids, and when his father got like that he used to weep and shout and wave his hands, but that was only now and then. He was gas, too, though not, Denis gathered, great gas. Willy suddenly waved his hands and shouted something in a foreign language.

"What's that?" asked Denis with the deepest admiration.

"German," Stein replied, in his graceless way.

"What does it mean?" asked Denis.

"I dunno," Stein said lightly.

Denis was disappointed. For a fellow like himself, who was interested in tanks, a spatter of German might one day be useful. He had the impression that Stein was only letting on to remember parents he had lost before he was really old enough to remember them.

Their talk was interrupted by Father Houlihan, a tall, morose-looking priest. He had a bad belly and a worse temper, but Denis knew Father Houlihan liked him, and he admired Father Houlihan. He was violent, but he wasn't a stinker.

"Hah!" he said, in his mocking way. "And what do you two cock sparrows think you're doing out here?"

"We're excused, Father," Denis said brightly, leaping to his feet.

"No one is excused anything in this place till I excuse him," snarled Father Houlihan cheerfully, "and I don't excuse much. Run in to Mass now, ye pair of heathens!"

"But we're Protestants, Father!" Stein cried, and Denis was half afraid of seeing the red flush on Father Houlihan's forehead that showed he was out for blood.

"Aha, what fine Protestants we have in ye!" he snorted good-humoredly. "I suppose you have a Protestant sling-shot in your pocket this very minute, you scoundrel, you!"

"I have not!" Stein shouted. "You know Murphy took it off me."

"Mr. Murphy to you, Willy Stein," said the priest, pinching his ear playfully and pushing him toward the chapel. "And next time I catch you with a slingshot I'll give you a Catholic cane on your fat Protestant backside."

The two boys went into chapel and sat together on a bench at the back. Willy was muttering indignantly to himself, but he waited until everyone was kneeling with bowed head. Then, to Denis's horror, he took out a sling-shot and a bit of paper, which he chewed up into a wet ball. There was nothing hasty or spontaneous about this. Stein went about it with a concentration that was almost pious. As the bell rang for the Consecration, there was a ping, and a seminarist kneeling at the side of the chapel put his hand to his ear and looked angrily round. But by this time Stein had thrown himself on his knees, and his eyes were shut in a look of rapt devotion. It gave Denis quite a turn. Even if he wasn't a Catholic, he had been brought up to respect every form of religion.

The business of going to Mass and feeling out of it made Denis Halligan completely fed up with being a Proddy. He had never liked it anyway, even at home, as a kid. He was gregarious, and a born gang leader, a promoter of organization, and it cut him to the heart to feel that at any moment he might be deserted by his gang because, through no fault of his own, he was not a Catholic and might accidentally say or do the wrong thing. He even resented the quiet persuasion that the school authorities exercised on him. A senior called Hanley, whom Nigel described sarcastically as "Halligan's angel," was attached to Denis—not to proselytize but to give him an intelligent understanding of the religious life of the group. Hanley had previously been attached to Stein, but that had proved hopeless, because Stein seemed to take Hanley's company as a guarantee of immunity from punishment, so he merely involved Hanley in every form of forbidden activity, from smoking to stealing. One day when Stein stole a gold tiepin from a master's room, Hanley had to report him. On Hanley's account, he was not flogged but told to put the tiepin back in the place from which he had taken it. Stein did so, and seized the opportunity to pinch five shillings instead, and this theft was discovered only when someone saw Stein fast asleep in bed with his mouth open and the two half crowns in his jaw. As Hanley, a sweet and saintly boy, said to Denis, it wasn't Stein's fault. He was just unbalanced.

In any other circumstances Denis would have enjoyed Hanley's attention, but it made him mad to be singled out like this and looked after like some kid who couldn't undo his own buttons.

"Listen, Hanley," he said angrily one day when he and Nigel were discussing football and Hanley had slipped a little homily into the conversation. "It's no good preaching at me. It's not my fault that I'm a Proddy."

"Well, you don't have to be a Proddy if you don't want to be," Hanley said with a smile. "Do you?"

"How can I help it?" asked Denis.

"Well, who'd stop you?"

"My mother would, for one."

"Did you try?"

"What do you mean, Hanley?"

"I mean, why don't you ask her?" Hanley went on, in the same bland way. "I wouldn't be too sure she wants you to be a Proddy."

"How could I ask her?"

"You could write. Or phone," Hanley added hastily, seeing the look on Denis's face at the notion of writing an extra letter. "Father Houlihan would let you use the telephone, if you asked him. Or I'll ask him, if you like."

"Do if you want to," said Denis. "I don't care."

He didn't really believe his mother would agree to something he wanted, just like that, but he had no objection to a free telephone call that would enable him to hear her voice again. To his astonishment, she made no difficulty about it.

"Why, of course, darling," she said sweetly. "If that's how you feel and Father Houlihan has no objection, I don't mind. You know I only want you to be happy at school."

It was a colossal relief. Overnight, his whole position in the school changed. He had ceased to be an outsider. He was one of the gang. He might even be Chief Gang Leader in the course of time. He was a warmhearted boy, and he had the feeling that by a simple gesture he had conferred an immense benefit on everybody. The only person who didn't seem too enthusiastic was Father Houlihan, but then he was not much of an enthusiast anyway. "My bold young convert," he said, pulling Denis's ear, "I suppose any day now you'll start paying attention to your lessons."

Yet the moment he had made his decision, he began to feel guilty about young Stein. As has been said, he was not only gregarious, but he was also a born gang leader, and had the feeling that someone might think he had deserted an ally to secure his own advantage. He was suddenly filled with a wild desire to convert Willy as well so that the pair of them could be received as a group. He saw it as even more of a duty of Willy's than of his own. Willy had been saved from his parents' fate by a good kind Catholic family, and it was the least they could expect that Willy should show his gratitude to them, to the school, and to Ireland.

But Willy seemed to have a deplorable head for theology. All the time they talked, Denis had the impression that Willy was only planning some fresh mischief.

"Ah, come on, Willy," he said authoritatively, "you don't want to be a blooming old Proddy."

"I don't want to be a Cat either," said Willy with a shrug.

"Don't you want to be like the other fellows in the school?"

"Why don't they want to be like me?" asked Stein.

"Because there's only two of us, and there's hundreds of them. And they're right."

"And if there were hundreds of us and two of them, we'd be right, I suppose?" Stein said with a sneer. "You want to be like the rest of them. All right, be like the rest of them, but let me alone."

"I'm only speaking for your own good," Denis said, getting mad. What really made him mad was the feeling that somehow Stein wasn't speaking to him at all; that inside, he was as lonely and lost as Denis would have been in similar circumstances, and he wouldn't admit to it, wouldn't break down as Denis would have done. What he really wanted to do was to give Stein a sock in the gob, but he knew that even this was no good. Stein was always being beaten, and he always yelled bloody murder, and next day he came back and did the same thing again. Everyone was thinking exclusively of Stein's good, and it always ended up by their beating him, and it never did him any good at all.

Denis confided his difficulties to Hanley, who was also full of concern for Stein's good, but Hanley only smiled sadly and shook his head.

"I know more about that than you do, Denis," he said, in his fatherly way. "I'll tell you if you promise not to repeat it to a living soul."

"What is it?" asked Denis eagerly.

"Promise! Mind, this is serious!"

"Oh, I promise."

"The fact is that Stein isn't a Proddy at all," Hanley said sadly.

"But what is he?"

"Stein is a Jew," Hanley said in a low voice. "That's why his father and mother were killed. Nobody knows that, though."

"But does Stein know he's a Jew?" Denis asked excitedly.

"No. And mind, we're not supposed to know it, either. Nobody knows it, except the priests and ourselves."

"But why doesn't somebody tell him?"

"Because if they did, he might blab about it—you know, he's not very smart—and then all the fellows would be jeering at him. Remember, Denis, if you ever mentioned it, Father Houlihan would skin you alive. He says Stein is after suffering enough. He's sorry for Stein. Mind, I'm only warning you."

"But won't it be awful for him when he finds out?"

"When he's older and has a job, he won't mind it so much," said Hanley.

But Denis wasn't sure. Somehow, he had an idea that Stein wanted to stay a Proddy simply because that was what his father and mother had been and it was now the only link he had with them, and if someone would just tell him, he wouldn't care so much and would probably become a Catholic, like Denis. Afterward, when he did find out that everything he had done was mistaken, it might be too late. And this—and the fact that Father Houlihan, whom Denis admired, was also sorry for Willy Stein—increased his feeling of guilt, and he almost wished he hadn't been in such a hurry himself about being converted. Denis wasn't a bright student, but he was a born officer and he would never have deserted his men.

The excitement of his own reception into the Church almost banished the thought of Stein from his mind. On the Sunday he was received, he was allowed to sleep late, and Murphy, the seminarist, even brought him comics to read in bed. This was real style! Then he dressed in his best suit and went down to meet his mother, who arrived, with his sister Martha, in a hired car. For once, Martha was deferential. She was impressed, and the sight of the chapel impressed her even more. In front of the high altar there was an isolated prie-dieu for Denis himself, and behind him a special pew was reserved for her and his mother.

Denis knew afterward that he hadn't made a single false move. Only once was his exaltation disturbed, and that was when he heard the *ping* of a slingshot and realized that Stein, sitting by himself in the back row, was whiling away the time by getting into fresh mischief. The rage rose up in Denis, in spite of all his holy thoughts, and for a moment he resolved that when it was all over he would find Willy Stein and beat him into a jelly.

Instead, when it was over he suddenly felt weary. Martha had ceased to be impressed by him. Now she was just a sister a bare year younger who was mad with him for having stolen the attention of everybody. She knew only too well what a figure she would have cut as a convert, and was crazy with jealousy.

"I won't stand it," she said. "I'm going to be a Catholic, too."

"Well, who's stopping you?" Denis asked.

"Nobody's going to stop me," said Martha. "Just because Daddy is fond of you doesn't mean that I can't be a Catholic."

"What has Daddy to do with it?" asked Denis with a feeling of alarm.

"Because now that you're a Catholic, the courts wouldn't let him have you," Martha said excitedly. "Because Daddy is an atheist, or something, and he wanted to get hold of you. He tried to get you away from Mummy. I don't care about Daddy. I'm going to be converted, too."

"Go on!" growled Denis, feeling sadly how his mood of exaltation was fading. "You're only an old copycat."

"I am not a copycat, Denis Halligan," she said bitterly. "It's only that you always sucked up to Daddy and I didn't, and he doesn't care about me. I don't care about him, either, so there!"

Denis felt a sudden pang of terror at her words. In a

dim sort of way he realized that what he had done might have consequences he had never contemplated. He had no wish to live with his father, but his father came to the school to see him sometimes, and he had always had the feeling that if he ever got fed up with living at home with his mother and Martha, his father would always have him. Nobody had told him that by becoming a Catholic he had made it impossible for his father to have him. He glanced round and saw Stein, thin and pale and furtive, slouching away from the chapel with his hand in his pocket and clutching his slingshot. He gave Denis a grin in which there was no malice, but Denis scowled and looked away.

"Who's that?" asked Martha inquisitively.

"Oh, him!" Denis said contemptuously. "That's only a dirty Jew-boy."

Yet even as he spoke the words he knew they were false. What he really felt toward Willy Stein was an aching envy. Nobody had told him that by changing his faith he might be unfaithful to his father, but nobody had told Stein, either, and, alone and despairing, he still clung to a faith that was not his own for the sake of a father and mother he had already almost forgotten, who had been murdered half a world away and whom he would never see again. For a single moment Denis saw the dirty little delinquent whom everyone pitied and despised transfigured by a glory that he himself would never know.

from

New Lives: Survivors of the Holocaust Living in America

by Dorothy Rabinowitz

Elena and Stefan, Polish Holocaust
survivors who married in New York City
after the war, tell their bitter stories.
They both came from the same city,
Lodz. Elena describes what it was like in
the Lodz ghetto and then in Auschwitz.
Stefan can barely speak of the past.

Elena

My husband and I didn't have what you would call a wild
romance before we married. He had been in love with a
girl who did not survive, and I with a man who did not

come to the United States. I wanted time before we married, I wanted to think for a while, so I went to stay with my relatives in the Midwest while Stefan was getting himself settled in New York. My cousins were American-born Jews: very Middle Western, kind, generous people, who also shrank from me a little. You understand, the concentration camp experience is nothing that endears you to people. People who came to my cousins' house used to ask me such things as whether I had been able to survive because, perchance, I had slept with an SS man. And if I had, did they think I would tell them? There were difficulties all around in that visit, what with my cousin taking sick and me feeling very uncomfortable, so before the summer was over, I packed up and went back to New York, where Stefan and I were married right away. The truth is he was much lonelier than I was, and so he wanted the marriage more.

My husband came from the same city as I did, Lodz. They were people of means, his family, assimilationists. Stefan grew up thinking he was a Pole, that Poland was his country, because they had sent him to private schools from the time he was small. He was a patriot like all the rest of them in his classes—his heart pounded just like theirs when they sang their patriotic songs, and he never learned a word of Yiddish until he was in a concentration camp. My family were not people of such great means, not like Stefan's family, but we were comfortable. My father was an educator and a leading Zionist in Lodz. Stefan's father was a Zionist, too, a complete assimilationist and a Zionist; he had settled it all in his mind, somehow, these two things were compatible. After the Nazis invaded Poland, someone informed my father that the Jewish Agency in Palestine had sent some certificates for Poland's leading Zionists, to get them out of the country, and that the Germans were allowing it; and that set off long discussions at home. Getting out of Poland meant going from Lodz to Warsaw, and that meant going by train and taking off the yellow armband, because Jews were not permitted to travel anymore. My mother and father debated and argued, but my mother was better at it than my father. She didn't want to leave her things, her furniture. Had she listened to my father, we would have been out of Poland long before the Germans invaded. I knew people who had much more to lose than she did, people who fled. But my mother was devoted to her possessions, to the kind of life she had. It was already October 1939, and Mother and Father debated should they take off the yellow armband and go on the train, should they or shouldn't they go. They took two days to debate it, and they were no closer to an answer after two days, when it was too late, than they were when they began. There were five certificates of exit sent to Lodz. Of the five, two were for elderly men in their seventies. They could not flee, they said; whatever happened to all the Jews would happen to them. One was a younger man, in his forties, the same age as my father. He left; he was the only one who did. And when we were in the ghetto in 1940, and everywhere around us there were people dying of typhus and dysentery, we got a postcard from Trieste. It was from him, the one who left; he and his family were on their way to Palestine. When my mother read the postcard, she cried. "It's my fault," she told us. But by then it was too late to think about whose fault it was.

Two days later, my father received a summons from the Gestapo. It happened that the Gestapo offices were located in the Gymnasium where my father taught. Over the years, the Gymnasium had collected enough money to build a great modern building for its students, not just classrooms but a gym and tennis courts, and a field for ball games. In September of 1939 our family was supposed to move into this complex. The perfect month and year: The Germans arrived in September 1939. My father had transferred his office and safe to the new Gymnasium office already. In answer to the summons, he arrived at Gestapo headquarters, which was his own office, and was arrested by a Gestapo officer who sat behind my father's desk, with my father's papers in his hands. On the desk in front of him were the things from my father's safe. They arrested him because he was an intellectual.

We tried to keep our apartment, because the prison into which my father had been put was only two blocks away from it. Jews were only allowed to walk in the streets till five in the afternoon, and since food from Jewish women who had family in the prison was not accepted until four-thirty, you had to be very lucky to get to the gate and off the street in time. My mother was determined to stay near that prison. Because we had a very nice apartment, she was afraid the Germans would throw us out of it, so she made it as ugly as she could, and I helped her. We spread ashes on the floor, smeared the walls, and dirtied the whole place. By the time we had taken off the drapes and soiled the windows, it looked shabby, but it was still hard to hide the fact that it was a nice apartment. It was bleak, but it wouldn't pass for a hovel; there were too many windows, dirty or not, too much space. We were not thrown out until my father had been let out of prison, three months later, and then we had to go into the ghetto.

Before that, we saw very few SS. Mostly we were being pushed around and abused by the Wehrmacht, though occasionally you might find a decent soldier, too. Food was the greatest problem for us. The Germans couldn't tell I was Jewish, but the Poles always could. I don't know why, since my Polish was much better than that of the average Pole; my eyes were green, I had straight hair—I didn't look Jewish at all. One day my friend Sonia and I stood in line to get bread. There was a separate line for Jews and for Poles, and since there was a much better chance to get food on the Polish line, Sonia smuggled herself onto it. She had just got up to the window, and had her hand on the bread, when a Polish woman yelled, "Jew! Dirty Jew! What are you doing in our line?" The German soldier pulled Sonia by the shoulders and threw her into our line. We looked at each other, and then Sonia tried to smile at me, but she couldn't.

All along I went to school in the ghetto. Occasionally we would read for a whole day, or sometimes only for a few hours, depending on how cold it was. It got colder each day. It was bitter winter weather. We met for classes each day and went wherever we found some room that had not been requisitioned. Then, the next day, teachers would find that room had been taken, and overnight they would set up a class somewhere else. I can't say that we learned very much.

All this time, our family was getting privileged treatment. Certain people in the ghetto, and we were among them, got a special ration, people in key positions. It was unjust and my father knew it; he knew our extra share came from the communal rations. Rumkowski, the director of the ghetto, was a friend of my father, a *chaver*. My father got a double ration for himself, my mother, and for me, and even with it both my parents were emaciated. My father's prewar suit hung on him. He was the kind of man who was ashamed of getting the extra food. I saw the expression on his face when he talked about it. He knew that other people were getting much less. But the hunger was so terrible, who was so good and brave as to give up an extra ration? And how could you be so good and brave for your wife and children, too?

My father became very thin and yellow, anyway. When you don't eat, the skin becomes like parchment. My mother was just as hungry, but somehow she looked better than he did; she needed less. And I—I was blooming. I was sixteen and I was blooming. My mother used to give me a part of her bread. With the help we got from the Älteste der Juden, we survived the ghetto, but in August 1944 they told us they were going to relocate us. The German in charge, Hans Biebow,* came in and talked to us all, and said they wanted us to go to our relocation peacefully. Biebow opened up his coat and pointed inside. "See, I have no gun on me." That was what he told us to prove that we had nothing to fear from the move, but we didn't believe him. We ran; we all started to hide, but it was impossible: You can't hide without food. The moment you come to claim a ration there is no more hiding for you; to have a hiding place you have to prepare it, be sure you won't be denounced by the neighbors or the workmen whom you pay to help you prepare it. You had to have courage to make a hiding place and my parents just did not have the courage to hide or to run—to do anything.

*Hanged after 1945, for war crimes.

I was much younger when I judged my mother for being devoted to her possessions. When I became middle-thirtyish, I saw what middle age does to you. You slow down, you're just not in the same fighting mood as you were when you were younger. You hate to give up the familiar. I begin to understand her a little. But she was wrong. I resented her, yes, I was mad at her. Because those that were separated from their mothers at Auschwitz were better off. An older person was a burden; my mother was only forty-eight, but that, for the camps, was old. The truth is a terrible thing to say, isn't it?

We were caught in the middle of August. We were hiding in my father's office, and the child of a neighbor, who was hiding with us, cried. They heard us, we were caught. It doesn't really matter. If we hadn't been caught then, it would only have given us another two or three weeks in the ghetto. My father tried to guess where we were going; possibly he even knew, but he only told me to stay with my mother because probably they would separate the sexes. That was all he told me. When we got to Auschwitz, I stuck to my mother; I held on. The men were lined up apart from us. I thought that the Germans would separate you if they thought you were related, if you were mother and daughter, so I let go of my mother and I walked with the mother of my friend Gina, and Gina walked with my mother. I thought, if I walk with my own mother, they'll see the family resemblance. Gina's mother was a tiny gray-haired lady, but my mother was young looking and tall, a handsome woman. When we came up to the SS, Gina and my mother were in front of us. They were both waved to the left, where I saw mostly younger-looking people, and I wanted to go left, too; I didn't know what right meant. I had no idea. I wanted to go with my mother and Gina. When I came forward to the barrier, a blond, good-looking SS officer asked me, pointing to Gina's mother, *"Ist das deine Mutter?"* And I said, *"Nein."* I didn't have any reason to say she was my mother. *"Wie alt bist du?"* the German asked me. *"Acht-zehn,"* I said. He looked me up and down. *"Das ist alt genug,"* he said, waving me to the left. Gina's mother went to the right. If I hadn't been stopped and asked about the woman I was walking with, I would have been sent to the gas chamber with her. We stayed in Auschwtiz for five days, and then we were sent to a branch of Grossrosen, where they had an airplane factory. Five hundred of us from Lodz were put to work there, but there were also many foreign workers there, slave laborers and prisoners of war.

By this time the Germans had taken over Italy, so Germany and Italy were no longer allies. In the factory now there were Italian prisoners of war working along with us. Such kind, courageous men, those Italians! They helped us, and brought food to us at work. And though things were very bad for us, though we were hungry and we wore rags, our spirits were not so low in Grossrosen because of those Italian prisoners of war. We saw them every day at the factory, and though, since we were Jews, they were strictly forbidden to help us and speak to us, they did help us, they did speak to us. They helped us with food; they kept us alive with hope. They would get to us quietly when the SS women guards were not looking, or sometimes they diverted the attention of the guards by flirting with them. Some of those Italian men were very handsome, too. While one of them would flirt and take up the attention of the SS woman, another would smuggle some food to us, or just whisper, *"La guerra finita."* Or they would just say to us, in broken German, "Don't give up hope." If you knew what the behavior of those people meant to us, what those words meant to us!

In the camp itself, the SS woman in charge took a special dislike to my mother. Possibly it was because my mother was tall and nice-looking and you could see that she was a lady. One day, after her gallstones had left her in peace for seventeen years, my mother had a bad attack. The pain sent her to the infirmary—not that there was any medication there for us, but there was a Hungarian Jewish doctor, and at least, lying there, she didn't have to go to the factory. But I was young, and because I was young, I was shrewder and sharper; I knew it was no good to be in the infirmary. She stayed half a day, and I told her, "Mama, tomorrow get up, line up with us and go to work." But my mother still just could not understand where she was or what it was all about, and so she stayed there. The next afternoon, the SS Kommandoführerin who hated my mother came into the infirmary. She ran to the bed where my mother was lying and shouted at her, "I'm going to send you out on the next transport to Auschwitz! I don't need any rich lazy Jews here." And, in fact, the next day we were told we were being shipped out of Grossrosen. The Kommandoführerin said we were only going to another camp to work, but the other SS told us we were really going back to Auschwitz. They said that we were going directly to the gas chambers, that we were not even going to stop at the main camp first for a selection.

Then the Kommandoführerin put me and my mother with a group of about sixty women who had somehow miraculously managed to escape the death selection before this. One was lame, one had a bad eye, the rest were emaciated; two or three of the women were past forty. I was the only one in the group who was young and in good health. I said nothing to my mother; I stood with her, and I went with her, but I resented it: I couldn't let her go alone, and yet I didn't want to die. What I wanted was for my mother to tell me, "You stay, and I'll go; you don't have to come with me."

But she didn't. I wanted her to tell me that. I don't even know, if she'd said what I wanted, whether I would have stayed behind. Perhaps, if my mother had known for sure we were going to die, she would have said something to me; she would have sent me away from her. In the end, it turned out that we did only go to another camp, as the Kommandoführerin said. None of us ever knew anything for sure, because they mixed you up deliberately. We came to Belsen at night after a day or two on the train, and there I knew we could not survive. There was no work. All we did all day was sit there and kill lice, and beg or steal water for washing and drinking. The lice were brought in by the Hungarians, who were completely broken people, physically and spiritually. They had been rounded up only in the last year of the war; they didn't have the hardening of the ghetto experience. I tried to avoid them; I didn't hate them; they were pathetic, just living stinking skeletons who kept crying to God in Hungarian. Pretty soon we all had lice, and from the lice came the fever. Spotted typhoid killed my mother after she lay unconscious for days. I had the fever but was conscious most of the time; I remember everything. In the end, I gave up on my mother; I couldn't even lift her head. Before she died, while she was lying there, she made me swear to her that I would go to my uncle in America when the war was over. She was many things, my mother, there were many sides to her, but at the end her last breath was spent on me. She was thinking of me; I couldn't mistake that.

Stefan

I don't like to speak of the past. I had enough. Furthermore I wouldn't even go to a synagogue to say Kaddish for my father. It would be disrespectful to his memory. You see that synagogue there? People say, "Why don't you even go in and say Kaddish for your father?" Not a day passes, not a day, that I don't think of my father; should I go in there with those people and their furs and that atmosphere and pray for the memory of my father? First of all, I'm not a religious Jew, and if we had not had to have a bar mitzvah for my son, I wouldn't even belong to a synagogue. I was not bar-mitzvahed in Poland; we had an absolutely assimilated family. My father was a Zionist, and a leading one, too.

Oh, there are many things I cannot understand now. Why Father, who was such a passionate Zionist, wanted us to assimilate; not only that, many things. We never talked about it. Maybe he thought that assimilation is the way we would all survive in Europe. Poland was my country, I thought of it as my country; Polish was my language; Poland. I spit on Poland. Yes, probably that was what my father thought: Assimilation meant survival. I know I was dead many times; I crawled; but I still wanted to live. If I could talk to each one of those six million Jews that died, and could ask them, Do you want to die as a Jew or live as a Christian, ninety-five percent of them would choose to live, wouldn't they?

An American captain saved my life, a doctor from Brooklyn. The last few weeks of the war, I was put in a barracks with dying people. It was a camp near Mauthausen. They had given us poisoned food. It was one of the last-minute efforts to eliminate witnesses—Himmler's orders. I got sick with everyone else, and by the time the Americans came, I was one of those put on a stretcher and made ready to be removed to a mass grave. Then this Army doctor from Brooklyn noticed that I moved my leg, and I was taken off the stretcher and brought to a field hospital. He watched over me for four weeks, but when I woke up, delirious, and saw this uniform, I ranted and yelled at him like an insane man: "My father would still be alive now if the Americans hadn't waited for the Russians to advance on Berlin!"

My father. In the camps, fathers fought sons for food, and brother fought brother sometimes; I saw those things. But between me and my father there was nothing like that. There had always been a great warmth between us. When I was growing up, I know I would rather have talked to him than anybody, and he felt the same about me. One day in the camp, he took me aside and told me that he had witnessed my brother's death, and that I now must stay alive. He meant it. Then he gave me his bread and I took it. I took it because he showed me he would throw it away and not eat it himself if I didn't take it from him. I didn't cry when he died, though. I don't know why, but no tears ever came to me.

In 1946, I came to New York. I was twenty-four then. Those first two years here, I was so lonely. Sometimes it comes back to me now how I felt. I lived with my uncle, and almost every night after supper I would rush out of that house and into the street, because I couldn't stand hearing my cousins call "Ma" and "Pa" to my aunt and uncle. I had still never cried before that time, and the reason I cried then was my uncle found a letter written to him by my father in 1939, which he showed to me. It had been written during the time I was away in school. My father wrote about this and that in the letter, and then he wrote about me: "Stefan went to France and I don't have to tell you how lonely I am for him." He wrote how much he missed me, and when I heard that in my uncle's house in 1946, yes, I cried for the first time.

from

Fires in the Mirror: Crown Heights, Brooklyn, and Other Identities

by Anna Deavere Smith

This dramatic monologue is one of many in Anna Deavere Smith's Obie Award winner. In this piece she takes on the identity of Letty Cottin Pogrebin, one of the founders of *Ms.* magazine, who tells about her uncle Isaac, a Holocaust survivor.

Letty Cottin Pogrebin: Isaac

(Morning. Spring. On the phone. She is in her office in her home on West 67th Street and Central Park West in Manhattan. Her office has an old-fashioned wooden rolltop desk and bookcases filled with books. She says she was wearing leggings and a loose shirt.)

Well,
it's hard for me to do that
because
I think there's a tendency to make hay
with the Holocaust,
to push
all the buttons.
And I mean this story about my uncle Isaac—
    makes *me* cry
and it's going to make your audience cry
and I'm beginning to worry
that
we're trotting out our Holocaust stories
too regularly and that we're going to inure each other
    to the truth of
them.
But
I think
maybe if you let me read it,
I would prefer to read it:
(*Reading from* Deborah, Golda, and Me)

"I remember my mother's cousin
Isaac who came to New York
immediately after the war and lived with us for several
    months.
Isaac is my connection to dozens of other family
    members who
were murdered in the concentration camps.
Because he was blond and blue-eyed he had been
chosen as the designated survivor of his town.
That is the Jewish councils had instructed him to do
    anything
to stay alive and tell the story.
For Isaac
anything turned out to mean this.
The Germans suspected his forged Aryan papers and
    decided that he
would have to prove by his actions that he was not a
    Jew.
They put him on a transport train with the Jews of
    his town
and then gave him the task of herding into the gas
    chambers
everyone in his train load.
After he had fulfilled that assignment
with patriotic
German efficiency,
the Nazis accepted the authenticity of his identity
    papers
and let him go.
Among those whom Isaac packed into the gas
    chambers that day
dispassionately as if shoving a few more items into an
    overstuffed

closet
were his wife
and
two children.
The designated survivor
arrived in America
at about age forty
(*Breathes in*)
with prematurely white hair and a dead gaze within
    the sky blue
eyes that'd helped save his life.
As promised he told his story to dozens of Jewish
    agencies
and community leaders and to groups of families and
    friends which
is how I heard the account
translated from his Yiddish
by my mother.
For months he talked,
speaking the unspeakable.
Describing a horror
that American Jews had suspected but could not
    conceive.
A monstrous tale
that dwarfed the demonology of legend
and gave me the nightmare I still dream to this day.
And as he talked
Isaac seemed to grow older and older
until one night
a few months later
when he finished telling everything he knew
he died."

A Soldier's Letter Home
by Delbert D. Cooper

Delbert D. Cooper volunteered for the
U.S. Army in January 1943 and was sent
overseas two and a half months after he
was married. On May 5, 1945, Cooper's
71st Infantry Division was near Lambach,
Austria, when they received a report of
a concentration camp five kilometers
away. Since they had recently captured
a German supply train, they loaded up a
truck with food and drove to the camp.
The camp was Gunskirchen, although
they did not know its name at the time.

On the morning of May 6, 1945, Delbert
Cooper wrote this letter to his wife,
describing what he'd seen. He asked his
wife to type the letter and show it to
anyone she cared to because "it's the

truth as I saw it with my own eyes."

And he sent her the yellow star that one of the Jewish prisoners he freed had given to him.

In 1981 Delbert Cooper was a delegate to the International Liberators Conference in Washington, D.C. His original letter is in the collection of the Museum of Jewish Heritage in New York.

5/6/45
Austria

My dearest Joan:

Morning blondie, Here's that pest again. Guess it's been a couple of days since I wrote you. Can't keep track of the time anymore you know. Just days and nights now. The weather has been pretty bad for some time now. Rainy & cold, but I'm inside most of the time so it's not so bad.

I have seen the Alps mountains for the past couple of days. Reminds me of maneuvers.

You should see my clothes this morning. I rode on a jeep over these muddy roads yesterday and we didn't have any top on it. It was pulling a trailer and that thing really threw the mud. On top of that it was raining & the mud kinda spread out. Have to get some one of these women over here to wash it. The clothes, I mean.

Incidentally, I helped capture 8 Germans & one S.S. man yesterday. They are really beginning to give up. (4 hr. break.) Back again. Received some letters from you. Mar 23, April 9–10–11–12. Screwed up, eh. Received word the war was over a while ago, don't know for sure yet. When this is over there will probably be 3 choices for us. Army of occupation, CBI, or a discharge. Personally I'll take the latter of the three. Again your stamps came just in time. Was going to use the last one for this. Mailed two packages to you today. One with a flag & one with some coins & junk. Check. The packages didn't go out today. Tomorrow, maybe. Let you know when I write again.

Yesterday I was to a concentration camp. From what I saw with my own eyes, everything I ever heard about those places is absolutely true.

Here is how I happened to be there and a little about it.

The report came to us of this concentration camp being 5 kilometers down the road. It so happened that we had captured a whole German supply train the night before. So, 4 of us loaded up a truck with food & took it down. I'm going to tell you now I never want to see a sight again as we saw when we pulled in there. 1400 starving diseased, stinking people. It was terrible. Most of them were Jews that Hitler had put away for safekeeping. Some of them had been in camps for as long as 8 years. So help me, I cannot see how they stood it. No longer were most of them people. They were nothing but things that were once human beings. As we pulled off of the highway into the camp we had to shove them off of the truck. We had the first food that had been taken in there for a month. The people for the most part were dirty walking skeletons. Some were too weak to walk. They had had nothing to eat for so long. Some of them were still lying around dead where they had fallen. Others would fall as they tried to keep up with the truck. We were moving slow as we didn't want to run over anyone. We stopped to start to unload the food and then we really had a time. We tried & tried to keep them from crowding us so we could unload but they were just about beyond reasoning. Finally about four of them who spoke English started getting a little order for us. Even then we had to get off the truck & start shoving them out of the road. You could stand right in front of them & wave your arms for them to move over & they would just stand there, look right in your face and cry like a baby. It was really a pathetic scene. Finally we took out our guns & pointed them in their faces, but they still stood there and bawled. They were past being afraid of even a gun. We fired a few shots up in the air & still we couldn't clear them. They just couldn't believe that we had food for everyone. We pulled on farther back in to the camp after about half an hour, & the fellows who spoke English started getting some order.

Then we started to unload. We picked out about 15 to help us. How those skinny fellows ever lifted those boxes is beyond me. They were heavy for us to lift. But they got them off. While we were standing outside the truck, any number of them came up & touched us, as if they couldn't believe we were actually there. Some of them would try to kiss us even. (They must have been bad off.) Some of them would come up, grab you around the neck, & cry on your shoulder. Others would just look & cry. Some of them would throw their arms up in the air & pray. They were mostly the ones who were too weak to stand. I recall one woman who could only cry & point at her mouth. One fellow must have felt that he should give me something. As he had nothing to give of value, he gave me his little yellow star that designates a Jew. I'll send it to you in another letter. All of them wanted American cigarettes. I had given all of mine but 4 away on the road coming to the camp, so I halved the four so that eight of them could at least get a few puffs. Finally everything was unloaded. As the major who went with us couldn't get much order he left everything up to us 4 enlisted men. I estimated we had 2400 cans of chow aboard, so explained to one of the fellows to put two persons to a can. You see the condition these people were in—too much food all at once would probably have killed them. The cans were about the size of a regular can of peaches, so that was plenty for a starter. Someone, don't know who, had slipped 500 eggs aboard. I took one of the guys & told him to start with the children & give them one egg apiece & if he had any left over to give them to the women. The men, if you could call them that, could eat the meat. He told us people were dying at the average rate of 150 per day at this camp. They just stack them up in a pile if they died in the barracks. If they died outside they left them there. I know, I saw them.

There were 4 barracks for 1400 people. Room space was 1 yard per person. Just enough room to sit down. There were 2 latrines for 1400 people. Some of them were too weak to go to the latrines, so the barracks had to do. What a mess. There was human refuse every place. I had enough on my boots to be a walking sewer pipe. On top of all this, they had no water.

You see they had to stay off the roads so our supplies could keep rolling on. That was another thing we had to explain to them. Those that could walk wanted to travel & you can imagine how that would have been. The young people who were in this camp will probably never get over it. They will be stunted for life. You may see pictures of this back home as they put a call through for photographers to go there. Don't know whether they went or not as after we left we didn't go back. Instead, we got a better idea. Why truck the food in there when the tracks ran close by and we had a whole train of supplies. Also an engine with steam up and an Austrian engineer. So we moved the whole damned trainload down close to the camp. Enough food & other articles there to last them till they were strong enough to go on their way.

There are two things about all this that I want to tell you.

1. I never again want to see anything like that happen to anyone.
2. I wish 130 million American people could have been standing in my shoes.

You know, that SS man I captured later in the day never came so near to dying in his life. I pointed my pistol right against his head, but I just couldn't shoot him down in cold blood. Lost my nerve when I started squeezing the trigger. Too much like murder. If he would only have put up the littlest resistance he would now be a dead man.

Been having fun today. Went down to the P. W. cage & got about 8 Krauts to do some work. Don't think they didn't put out too. We made them do about everything. Hell, if one of them could have cut hair we'd have all gotten a haircut.

Well, honey, pretty tired after all that <u>work</u> today, so will bring this to a close. Be good, be better, you're the best.

Love,
Del

Show this to Mom, and anyone else you care to. It's all the truth as I saw it with my own eyes.

If you can't read this, please overlook it as I'm writing on the back of my mess kit.

Decided to write a little more.

Please do me a favor & you or Dad type up this complete letter for me. Want to show it to people when I come home. The details are still fresh in my mind as I write this. Probably forget a little of it by the time I come home. Also be very sure to keep the little yellow star if I send it.

Last night was Saturday. Did Mitzi guzzle that brew. I could have stood some after that hectic day of yesterday.

Close for sure now gal. Sun's down, it's getting dark, & I want to find my bed in the hay now. Gut Schlafen.*

Del

*Sleep well.

from

Night

by Elie Wiesel

This translation from the French by
Stella Rodway is the end of Wiesel's
stark autobiographical account of being
taken as a young boy with his family
and other Hungarian Jews to Auschwitz,
where he watched his father die. Then
the boy was sent on to Buchenwald.

On April tenth, there were still about twenty thousand of
us in the camp, including several hundred children. They
decided to evacuate us all at once, right on until the evening. Afterward, they were going to blow up the camp.

So we were massed in the huge assembly square, in rows
of five, waiting to see the gate open. Suddenly, the sirens
began to wail. An alert! We went back to the blocks. It
was too late to evacuate us that evening. The evacuation
was postponed again to the following day.

We were tormented with hunger. We had eaten nothing for six days, except a bit of grass or some potato peelings found near the kitchens.

At ten o'clock in the morning the SS scattered through the camp, moving the last victims toward the assembly place.

Then the resistance movement decided to act. Armed men suddenly rose up everywhere. Bursts of firing. Grenades exploding. We children stayed flat on the ground in the block.

The battle did not last long. Toward noon everything was quiet again. The SS had fled and the resistance had taken charge of the running of the camp.

At about six o'clock in the evening, the first American tank stood at the gates of Buchenwald.

Our first act as free men was to throw ourselves onto the provisions. We thought only of that. Not of revenge, not of our families. Nothing but bread.

And even when we were no longer hungry, there was still no one who thought of revenge. On the following day, some of the young men went to Weimar to get some potatoes and clothes—and to sleep with girls. But of revenge, not a sign.

Three days after the liberation of Buchenwald I became very ill with food poisoning. I was transferred to the hospital and spent two weeks between life and death.

One day I was able to get up, after gathering all my strength. I wanted to see myself in the mirror hanging on the opposite wall. I had not seen myself since the ghetto.

From the depths of the mirror, a corpse gazed back at me.

The look in his eyes, as they stared into mine, has never left me.

Today we have breaking of hearts.

Yesterday

We had ethnic cleansing. And tomorrow

morning

We shall have what to do after firing

the village.

But today we have breaking of hearts.

Refugees

Queue at the borders of all of the

neighboring countries,

And today we have breaking of

hearts. . . .

—from "Lessons of the War"
by Simon Rae
from *Klaonica: Poems for Bosnia*

Bibliography

Wherever they burn books, they will

also in the end burn human beings.

—Heinrich Heine

Bachrach, Susan D. *Tell Them We Remember: The Story of the Holocaust*. Boston: Little, Brown, 1994.
This outstanding photo-history, produced in association with the U.S. Holocaust Memorial Museum, focuses on what happened to young people whose world of family and friends, school and play was destroyed. Chosen as *Booklist*'s Top of the List for Youth Nonfiction in 1994.

Bierman, John. *Righteous Gentile: The Story of Raoul Wallenberg, Missing Hero of the Holocaust*. New York: Viking, 1981.
This account documents the wealthy, influential Swedish diplomat's efforts to save one hundred thousand Hungarian Jews and investigates his mysterious disappearance in 1945.

Butterworth, Emma Macalik. *As the Waltz Was Ending*. New York: Four Winds, 1984; Scholastic/Point, 1991, paper.
Butterworth, now a U.S. citizen, recalls six years of her Catholic girlhood in war-torn Vienna. Her anti-Nazi father is conscripted. Jewish friends are persecuted. When the Russians enter Vienna, Emma is raped.

Chaikin, Miriam. *A Nightmare in History: The Holocaust 1933–1945*. Boston: Houghton/Clarion, 1987.
Illustrated with searing documentary photographs, this stark, readable account introduces the history of anti-Semitism, the rise of Hitler, the Warsaw Ghetto uprising, the death camps, and the enduring consequences.

Dawidowicz, Lucy S. *The War Against the Jews, 1933–1945*. New York: Holt/Free Press, 1975; Bantam, 1986, paper.
This long, authoritative history of Nazi destruction of European Jewry describes the rise of anti-Semitism, the genocide, and the ways in which Jews and the rest of the world reacted to this systematic annihilation.

Epstein, Helen. *Children of the Holocaust*. New York: Putnam, 1979; Viking/Penguin, 1988, paper.
Epstein discusses how the experiences of concentration camp survivors have become a disturbing heritage for their children, who feel the parents' survivor guilt and the driving need to compensate for all that has been lost.

Fink, Ida. *A Scrap of Time and Other Stories*. Madeline Levine and Francine Prose, tr. New York: Pantheon, 1987; Schocken, paper; Northwestern University Press, 1995.
Many of these Holocaust stories about young survivors tell of the moments when Nazi terror invaded ordinary homes. Spare but powerful short fiction. Fink's novel *The Journey* (Farrar, Straus, 1992) is an intense story of two young Jewish sisters who flee the ghetto in disguise in 1942 and try to survive in wartime Germany. They find enemies and informers and also rare friendship.

Frank, Anne. *Anne Frank: The Diary of a Young Girl*. B. M. Mooyaart, tr. New York: Doubleday, 1952, rev. ed. 1967; Pocket/Washington Square, 1985, paper.
The classic journal, kept by Jewish teenager Anne during the two years she, her family, and several others hid from the Nazis in a secret annex in Holland.

Friedman, Carl. *Nightfather*. Arnold and Erica Pomerans, tr. New York: Persea, 1994.
In an autobiographical novel, a young girl in the Netherlands in the 1950s and '60s tells how her father's stories of his experience in the concentration camps are part of family life.

Friedman, Ina R. *The Other Victims: First-Person Stories of Non-Jews Persecuted by the Nazis*. Boston: Houghton, 1990.
Survivors of "undesirable" Gentile groups persecuted by the Nazis—including Gypsies, homosexuals, Jehovah's Witnesses, artists, political dissenters, the disabled, and kidnapped foreign workers—tell their stories. The facts are riveting and not easily available elsewhere.

Gehrts, Barbara. *Don't Say a Word*. Elizabeth D. Crawford, tr. New York: Macmillan/Margaret K. McElderry, 1986.
An autobiographical novel about an anti-Nazi Gentile family in a Berlin

suburb quietly portrays their mounting suffering under tyranny, as teenage Anna's father is arrested by the Gestapo, her brother dies in battle, and her Jewish girlfriend commits suicide with her family.

Gies, Miep, and Alison Leslie Gold. *Anne Frank Remembered: The Story of the Woman Who Helped to Hide the Frank Family*. New York: Simon & Schuster, 1987; Touchstone, 1988, paper.
Gies hid Anne Frank and her family, and this affecting memoir adds fresh perspective to the classic diary.

Gilbert, Martin. *The Holocaust: The History of the Jews of Europe During the Second World War*. New York: Holt, 1986; Holt/Owl, 1987, paper.
Gilbert draws on records and the testimonies of survivors to produce an accessible, massive, detailed chronological overview of the attempt to annihilate the Jews of Europe.

Greenfeld, Howard. *The Hidden Children*. New York: Ticknor & Fields, 1993.
Greenfeld interviews thirteen men and women who were hidden from the Nazis as children. They had to learn to lie, to conceal their true identities. Many were hidden by strangers, in convents and orphanages, in attics and underground passageways.

Hersey, John R. *The Wall*. New York: Knopf, 1951; Random/Vintage, 1988, paper.
A long, harrowing, ultimately triumphant novel of the heroic resistance of a group of Jews facing death under the Nazis in the Warsaw Ghetto.

Keneally, Thomas. *Schindler's List*. New York: Simon & Schuster, 1982; Touchstone, 1993, paper.
A novel based on the life of a German business owner who shielded his Jewish workers in Poland from death in Nazi concentration camps. Steven Spielberg has made a powerful film based on this story.

Kerr, Judith. *When Hitler Stole Pink Rabbit*. New York: Coward, 1977; Dell/Yearling, 1987, paper.
Based on the author's own experiences as a child, this story tells how a German Jewish girl and her family left their home in Berlin just before Hitler came to power in 1933. The sequel, *The Other Way Round*, describes their difficult adjustment in England.

Kerr, M. E. *Gentlehands*. New York: Harper, 1978; Harper/Trophy, 1990, paper.
In one of the great young adult novels, teenage Buddy tries to impress a rich, beautiful girl by taking her to visit his grandfather. Buddy's father has never had much to do with the old man, who lives alone in a big, elegant house with books and paintings and antiques, and is kind to animals. Then Buddy discovers that the grandfather he has come to know and admire is a Nazi war criminal.

Kertész, Imre. *Fateless*. Christopher C. Wilson and Katharina M. Wilson, tr. Evanston, Ill.: Northwestern University Press, 1992, paper.
Written from the point of view of a teenager, both innocent and immensely

experienced, this autobiographical novel, translated from the Hungarian, strips everything away and shows how a boy survived in the shadows of the chimneys.

Koehn, Ilse. *Mischling, Second Degree: My Childhood in Nazi Germany*. New York: Greenwillow, 1977; Penguin/Puffin, 1990, paper.
For her own protection in Nazi Germany, Ilse Koehn's parents kept from her that she was part Jewish. In diary form she tells of joining the Hitler Youth movement and of the two years she spends in a paramilitary girls' camp in occupied territory. A vivid, immediate account of what it was like to be a young German at that time.

Langer, Lawrence L., ed. *Art from the Ashes: A Holocaust Anthology*. New York: Oxford, 1995.
In this great collection for older readers, an eminent Holocaust scholar brings together personal accounts, art, drama, and poetry about the Holocaust.

Lanzmann, Claude. *Shoah: An Oral History of the Holocaust*. New York: Pantheon, 1985.
In this text of a landmark film, survivors talk about their experiences; so do the officers and engineers who ran the camps.

Leitner, Isabella. *Fragments of Isabella: A Memoir of Auschwitz*. New York: Crowell, 1978; Dell, 1983, paper.
In a haunting, impressionistic account of her brutal experiences, Leitner conveys what she and her sisters endured after they were rounded up as teenagers and transported to the Polish extermination camp, a story she continues in *Saving the Fragments*. Leitner's spare, simplified version, *The Big Lie: A True Story* (Scholastic, 1992), is for younger readers.

Levi, Primo. *The Drowned and the Saved*. Raymond Rosenthal, tr. New York: Summit, 1988; Random/Vintage, 1989, paper.
Discussing what it was like in the transports, the camps, even the crematoria, an Auschwitz survivor talks with candor about the enduring questions of guilt and survival. In all his books, such as the classic *If This Is a Man (Survival in Auschwitz)* and *The Reawakening*, Levi bears eloquent witness.

Levoy, Myron. *Alan and Naomi*. 1977; Harper/Trophy, 1987, paper.
Alan, a young Jewish American boy in New York during World War II, is reluctant at first to befriend Naomi, a Jewish refugee from France whose terrible experiences have left her seriously disturbed. A bleak, powerful novel about a young person's struggle to find meaning in the overwhelming evil of the Holocaust.

Lowry, Lois. *Number the Stars*. New York: Houghton, 1989; Dell, 1992, paper.
This novel of two Danish girls, one Jewish, the other not, highlights the way Danes protected their Jewish citizens from the invading Nazis. 1990 Newbery Medal winner.

Meltzer, Milton. *Never to Forget: The Jews of the Holocaust*. New York: Harper, 1976; Harper/Trophy, 1991, paper.
A compact, powerful, intensely human history of the Nazi extermination of the Jews.

Meltzer, Milton. *Rescue: The Story of How Gentiles Saved Jews in the Holocaust*. New York: HarperCollins, 1988, paper.

Drawing heavily on personal accounts, Meltzer looks back at the brave people—ordinary men, women, and children, priests, even whole villages—who risked their lives to aid the Jews.

Mumford, Erika. "The White Rose: Sophie Scholl, 1921–1943." In *The Music of What Happens: Poems That Tell Stories*. Sel. by Paul B. Janeczko. New York: Orchard, 1988.

A long dramatic poem based on the true story of the student resistance movement called the White Rose. Hans and Sophie Scholl, who organized the group in 1941, were caught and executed. Read this with Hermann Vinke's *The Short Life of Sophie Scholl* (HarperCollins, 1984).

Orlev, Uri. *The Island on Bird Street*. Hillel Halkin, tr. Boston: Houghton, 1984.

Set in the Warsaw Ghetto, Orlev's novel portrays the experiences of a young boy who escaped a Nazi roundup and waits steadfastly for his father to return.

————. *The Man from the Other Side*. Hillel Halkin, tr. Boston: Houghton, 1991.

Through the maze of filthy sewers under Nazi-occupied Warsaw, teenage Marek has to help his rough Polish stepfather smuggle food and arms to the desperate Jews in the walled-up ghetto. Orlev's fast-paced thriller is also about moral conflict, courage, and betrayal.

Ozick, Cynthia. *The Shawl*. New York: Knopf, 1983.

This searing story of camp suffering was awarded first prize in the O. Henry Prize Stories in 1981 and was included in *Best American Short Stories* of that year. It is published in a small book with a companion novella, *Rosa*.

Plant, Richard. *The Pink Triangle: The Nazi War against Homosexuals*. New York: Holt, 1988, paper.

Plant frames his history of the Nazi attempt to exterminate gay men with the poignant story of his own flight from Germany and his return more than thirty years later.

Rabinowitz, Dorothy. *New Lives: Survivors of the Holocaust Living in America*. New York: Knopf, 1976.

Survivors tell their bitter stories of the ghettos and the camps, though some can hardly bear to speak about what they remember.

Reichel, Sabine. *What Did You Do in the War, Daddy? Growing up German*. New York: Hill & Wang, 1989.

In a desperate attempt to come to terms with her shame and fury about the Nazi past, German Reichel (who now lives in the U.S.) talked to her parents and others of their generation and confronted her own memories of home and school in a post–World War II Germany that repressed its guilt.

Reiss, Johanna. *The Upstairs Room*. New York: Crowell, 1972; Harper/Trophy, 1990, paper.

With the honesty of Anne Frank, the author recalls her childhood experiences in hiding from the Germans who occupied her native Holland in World War II. She makes us imagine what it was like to be confined for over two years in a small, cramped room.

Richter, Hans P. *Friedrich*. Edite Kroll, tr. New York: Holt, 1970; Penguin/ Puffin, 1987, paper.
An unforgettable story of the persecution of the Jews in Nazi Germany, and how it affected two families, one Jewish, the other not.

Rogasky, Barbara. *Smoke and Ashes: The Story of the Holocaust*. New York: Holiday, 1988, paper.
Passionate and controlled, Rogasky's detailed history combines eyewitness accounts, statistics, and commentary. The eighty graphic photographs, many of them taken by Nazis at the time, add to the power of this account.

Siegal, Aranka. *Upon the Head of the Goat: A Childhood in Hungary, 1939–1944*. New York: Farrar, Straus, 1981; Penguin/Puffin, 1994, paper.
A memoir that documents the destruction of Siegal's family at the hands of the Nazis. At the end they are on the train to Auschwitz. The book was adapted into a memorable filmstrip distributed by Random/McGraw-Hill Educational Resources.

Spiegelman, Art. *Maus: A Survivor's Tale*. New York: Pantheon, 1986, paper.
In this candid autobiography and its brilliant 1991 sequel, *Maus II*, Spiegelman shows himself being told about the Holocaust by his Polish survivor father. Spiegelman not only explores the concentration camp experience, but also the guilt, love, and anger between father and son.

Strom, Yale. *A Tree Still Stands: Jewish Youth in Eastern Europe Today*. New York: Philomel, 1990.
"A kind of leftover people." An elegiac tone pervades these photo-essays of contemporary Jewish young people, aged seven to twenty, in East Germany, Poland, Czechoslovakia, Russia, Bulgaria, Yugoslavia, and Hungary. All are descendants of parents and grandparents who somehow managed to survive the Holocaust.

Vishniac, Roman. *A Vanished World*. New York: Farrar, Straus, 1983.
In his photographic documentary of ghetto life in Poland just prior to World War II, Vishniac reveals unemployed, boycotted, impoverished, pious people trying to carry on their familiar way of life—just before most of them were lost to the Nazi death camps.

Vos, Ida. *Hide and Seek*. Terese Edelstein and Inez Smidt, tr. Boston: Houghton, 1991.
Why must Rachel wear a yellow star? Why must she leave her parents? This autobiographical story about a young girl's experience under the Nazi occupation is told in a series of spare vignettes.

Wiesel, Elie. *The Night Trilogy: Night, Dawn, The Accident*. Stella Rodway, tr. New York: Hill & Wang, 1987, paper.

In *Night*, a stark autobiographical account, Wiesel describes the nightmare of being taken as a young boy with his father and other Hungarian Jews to the Auschwitz concentration camp, where he watched his father die.

This list is only a selection of the many great books written about the Holocaust and its aftermath. It is updated from an annotated bibliography first published in the June 1, 1989, special issue of *Booklist*, "Remembering the Holocaust."

Acknowledgments

Cooper, Delbert "A Soldier's Letter Home." Gift of Delbert Cooper, Yaffa Eliach Collection, donated by the Center for Holocaust Studies to the Museum of Jewish Heritage. Reprinted by permission.

Fink, Ida "Splinter," from *A Scrap of Time and Other Stories*, © 1995 by Northwestern University Press. Reprinted by arrangement with Liepman AG, c/o Joan Daves Agency as agent for the proprietor.

Friedman, Carl "No End," "Questions," from *Nightfather* by Carl Friedman, translated from the Dutch by Arnold and Erica Pomerans, © 1994 by Persea Books. Reprinted by permission of Persea Books.

Lanzmann, Claude "Abraham Bomba," "Franz Suchomel, SS Unterscharführer," "Raul Hilberg," from *Shoah* by Claude Lanzmann, © 1985 by Claude Lanzmann. Reprinted by permission of Georges Borchardt, Inc., for the author.

Leitner, Isabella from *The Big Lie: A True Story* by Isabella Leitner with Irving A. Leitner, © 1992 by Isabella Leitner. Reprinted by permission of Scholastic, Inc.

Levi, Primo "On the Bottom," "The Events of the Summer," from *If This Is a Man (Survival in Auschwitz)* by Primo Levi, translated from the Italian by Stuart Woolf; translation © 1959 by Orion Press, Inc., © 1958 by Giulio Einaudi editors S.p.A. Used by permission of Viking Penguin, a division of Penguin Books USA, Inc.

Mumford, Erika from "The White Rose: Sophie Scholl 1921–1943," by Erika Mumford © 1988 by David Mumford. Originally published in *Willow Water*, Every Other Thursday Press. Used by permission of David Mumford and Every Other Thursday Press.

O'Connor, Frank "A Minority," from *Collected Stories* by Frank O'Connor, © 1957 by Frank O'Connor. Reprinted by permission of Alfred A. Knopf, Inc., and by arrangement with Harriet O'Donovan Sheehy, c/o Joan Daves Agency as agent for the proprietor. Originally appeared in *The New Yorker*.

Ozick, Cynthia "The Shawl," from *The Shawl* by Cynthia Ozick, © 1980, 1983 by Cynthia Ozick. Reprinted by permission of Alfred A. Knopf, Inc. Originally appeared in *The New Yorker*.

Rabinowitz, Dorothy "Elena," "Stefan," from *New Lives: Survivors of the Holocaust Living in America* by Dorothy Rabinowitz, © 1976 by Dorothy

Sources of Additional Quotes

Heine, Heinrich *Almansor*. 1823. I.245. Translated from German.

Mathabane, Mark *Kaffir Boy*. New York: Macmillan, 1986.

Niemöller, Martin (1892–1984), German theologian. *Congressional Record*, October 14, 1968, p. 31636.